# PELARGONIUMS

■ For Colour and Variety ■

## Jan Taylor

First published in 1990 by
The Crowood Press Ltd
Ramsbury, Marlborough
Wiltshire SN8 2HR

This impression 1993

**British Library Cataloguing in Publication Data**

Taylor, Jan *1938–*
    Pelargoniums.
    I. Gardens. Geraniums & pelargoniums. Cultivation
    I. Title
    635.9'33216

    ISBN 1 85223 278 1

**Picture Credits**
All colour photographs by Frank and Jan Taylor, except those by the
following, to whom thanks are due: John Baker, for Figs 22, 30, 86 and 89;
Peter van Baaren, for Figs 10 and 50. Figs 31, 32 and 92 are reproduced
with the kind permission of Breeders Seeds

Fig 1 appearing on page 4 is F1 Hybrid, 'Pulsar Salmon'.

Colour artwork by Claire Upsdale-Jones

Typeset by Chippendale Type, Otley, West Yorkshire.
Printed and bound by Times Publishing Group, Singapore.

# Contents

# Introduction

Why are the names 'pelargonium' and 'geranium' so often confused? Although many people are quite happy with the term *'Pelargonium'*, there are some who are not familiar with it and, although they are actually growing pelargoniums as greenhouse or conservatory plants, in the garden, or on the patio in pots, urns and tubs, they call them 'geraniums'. This misnaming stems from a variety of reasons, and the grower probably is unaware of his or her mistake. Beginners alone cannot be blamed for this error as there are many notable parks, gardens, specialist nurseries and even committed enthusiasts who insist on saying 'geranium', and all one can do is follow suit. Indeed, the newcomer to gardening often feels uneasy using botanical names (although 'geranium' itself is a botanical name) and the term *Pelargonium is* a bit of a mouthful. Finally, people can be confused by idiosyncrasies within the naming system itself – Regal Pelargoniums are widely called pelargoniums and yet Zonal Pelargoniums, Ivy-leaved Pelargoniums and Scented-leaved Pelargoniums are commonly called 'geraniums'; the species, of course, should be known as *Pelargonium*.

When did this awful mix-up begin? Two hundred or so years ago botanists began to create a system of naming and classifying plants known as nomenclature or taxonomy. However, this early system was fairly rudimentary and many of its classifications were inaccurate. The family name for 'geraniums' and pelargoniums was *Geraniaceae*, and so the name 'geranium' stuck for them both. The *Pelargonium* was later regrouped into a section, or more correctly, a genus. Since those early days, botanists have updated or reclassified these sections, with the most recent completed work being undertaken in the 1960s. And at present, Professor van der Walt and his team at Stellenbosch University in South Africa are involved with more updating which has given rise to some re-classification of *Pelargonium* species. In this same family are four more types of plants, namely *Sarcocaulon, Monsonia, Erodium* and *Geranium*. The *Geranium* grows mainly in the northern hemisphere, so it is

*Fig 2 P.triste, the first species recorded blooming in Britain. It has fluffy carrot-like leaves and cream flowers with variable maroon markings; the flowers are night-scented.*

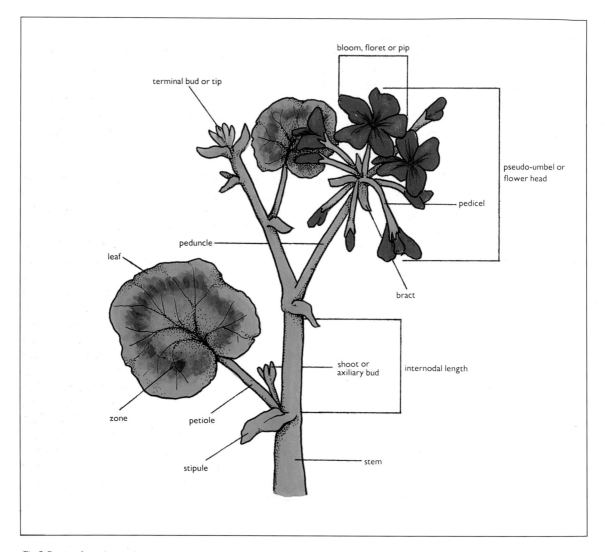

Fig 3 Parts of a pelargonium.

usually a very hardy plant, sometimes herb-aceous or evergreen, either a perennial or occasionally annual and cultivated in gardens on a rockery, in a scree or in the border, depend-ing on its stature. It is a fairly trouble-free plant with a few *Geranium* growing wild in Britain. Readers will be familiar with the beautiful blue blooms of *Geranium pratense* which grace our hedgerows and meadowlands and are now becoming more widespread on roadside verges and motorway reservations. Commonly called 'meadow cranesbill', it makes an excellent plant for the garden.

At this point, it would be opportune to give the reader a little insight into the use of botanical Latin. This is an internationally accepted method used to describe and name plants. Every species of plants is classified by two words, known as the binominal. The first word is that common to all species within a related group and is

6

known as the genus. This word should always be written with an initial capital, as in *Pelargonium*. The second part of the plant's binominal is unique to that species, like *Pelargonium zonale*, and lower case letters should be used. There may be one other word in the name, sometimes more, which could be a description of the plant's origin, form, habit and so on, for example *Pelargonium zonale* 'alba'. Sometimes this last word is named after the person who discovered the plant or someone to whom it is dedicated, for example, *P. Schottii* (named after Schott), so the word must begin with a capital letter. If, however, it is an explanation of a notable feature, such as '*reptans*' (creeping), then the word would begin with a small letter. These words are botanical Latin and should be printed in italics or underlined when written or typed. If the same genus is being used repeatedly and in close succession, frequently only the first letter of the genus is used, as in *P.zonale*. Common names are identified by the use of a small letter and inverted commas, as when 'geranium' is used as the common name for *Pelargonium*.

When cultivars (varieties cultivated by man) are listed, like in *Pelargonium zonale* 'Paul Crampel', the variety or cultivar name 'Paul Crampel' *should* be inside inverted commas, but often nursery catalogues, magazines and so on, omit these, which is a fairly acceptable practice.

The *Pelargonium* is without doubt the most popular genus of the family and is itself sub-divided into four groups:

(1) Specie Pelargoniums, including primary hybrids, Scented-leaved and Unique types.
(2) Regal Pelargoniums, including Dwarf Regals and Angel types and hybrids of the Regal.
(3) Zonal Pelargoniums. This is the largest group, whose plants are commonly called 'geraniums'. They can possess single, semi-double or double flowers. Some are miniature or dwarf-growing. Others have attractively marked or coloured foliage. The modern F1 Hybrid is a zonal type.
(4) Ivy-leaved Pelargoniums, including the hybrids between Ivy-leaved and Zonals. The blooms may be single, semi-double or double.

The name *Pelargonium* is derived from the Greek word, *pelargos*, meaning a stork and the plant was given this name on account of the shape of the fruit or seed head just before it is ripe and ready to disperse. Before this, the bloom must be fertilised in nature either by insects, rain, small animals, or perhaps a light breeze if the plants are colonised. The plant's pollen will be transferred to another compatible plant or even to its own receptive reproductive parts, then the ovary will swell and in a few days the set of fruits or seeds will be noticeable. Usually, there are five seeds placed around a column called a style or rostrum. On ripening, the seeds and the rostrum will become dry and light brown in colour. The seeds, while still in their case, will begin to curl from the base of the rostrum in an upward movement, finally being fixed to the tip for varying lengths of time until the conditions are suitable for them to detach themselves singly. The individual seeds are packed in a casing with a 'tail' called an awn which has long hairs that look like plumes when dispersal is imminent. On dispersal the awn will corkscrew to varying degrees, according to the humidity levels of the vicinity. The drier the area the better and further the seed will be distributed and, with the aid of the feathers on the spiralling awn, an individual seed (still in its casing) may be carried quite a distance from the seed parent. The central rostrum remains on the plant until it finally dries and falls away, when it can be carried on the fur or wool of grazing animals, or blown away on the wind. The seeds themselves are normally light brown or russet in colour,

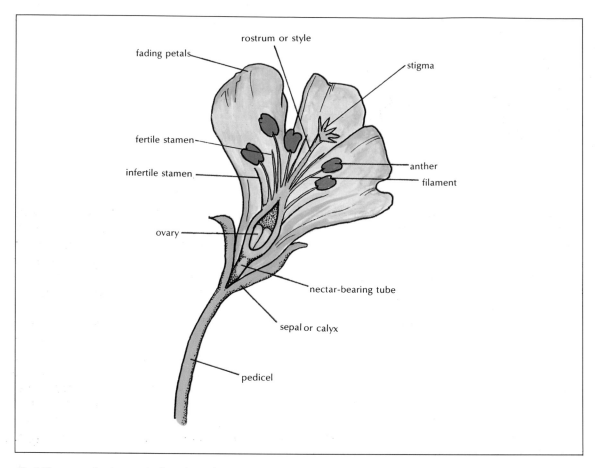

Fig 4 The reproductive parts of a pelargonium.

oval in shape with one end more pointed than the other and measure, depending on the species, from a minute pin-head size to ¼in (5mm) in length..

There are about 250 different species of *Pelargonium*, and almost all of these grow wild in Southern Africa on the edge of scrubland, stony and sandy areas where, when the rains *do* arrive, they do so in earnest. Some find the most dubious footholds in rocks on the plains, some scramble through shrubs, while some never see rain and survive on the moisture of night-time dews. There are also species to be found in Eastern Africa, Arabia, Syria, Madagascar and Western India and further south in Tristan da Cunha, Australia and New Zealand. One species, *P.cotyledonis*, remains a mystery and is only found growing wild on the island of St Helena.

The first *Pelargonium* is thought to have been introduced to Europe in 1632, when it was brought to England via Holland by John Tradescant. Records show it to have been in full bloom one year after arriving in England. We now know this plant as *Pelargonium triste*, but at that time it had the very descriptive name *Geranium indicum nocto odorato*; *indicum* because it was thought to have been found in India (although we now know that when the ships departed from India they stopped off at the Cape to replenish stores and acquire plant specimens); while *nocto odorato* simply means that it is night-scented. These delightful, night-scented *Pelargonium* species encourage moths and other nocturnal insects to visit the plant and collect pollen and so fertilise the blooms.

CHAPTER 1

# The Species

Most *Pelargonium* species are to be found growing naturally in certain areas in the southern hemisphere and mainly in Southern Africa. In suitable climates such as Spain, California and Italy they have also found their way from gardens into the wild.

All the species found to date have been grouped into sections. These sections are presently being reviewed at Stellenbosch University and from the work already completed it seems that they will be revised, but until that work is published in its entirety (there have been three volumes since 1977 dealing with about 150 of the 250 species), the sixteen sections listed below are those accepted by species enthusiasts and botanists since 1912.

*Hoarea, Seymouria, Polyactium, Otida, Ligularia, Jenkinsonia, Myrrhidium, Peristera, Camphylia, Dibrachya, Eumorpha, Glaucophyllum, Ciconium, Cortusina, Pelargonium* and *Isopetalum* (added when *P.cotyledonis* was removed from *Otida* to become the solitary specimen in *Isopetalum*).

It is impossible to generalise on the habit of *Pelargonium* species, so extreme are they in every way. Their roots are of three kinds: tuberous; fibrous; and tap rooted, which, of course, are adaptations of the plants' growing conditions in the wild. Tubers will store water during drought periods and have the storage powers to last through until the next rains. Tap roots seek far into crevices, searching for moisture and nutrients, which they store for short periods. Most gardeners are more familiar with fibrous roots, which are quite woody in

mature plants and sometimes grow horizontally, from which new plantlets, similar to suckers, can be formed. Fibrous-rooted *Pelargonium* grow in areas of moderate moisture and nutrient levels and are usually the more vigorous and most adaptable to growing conditions in Britain.

Foliage and forms are also diverse, ranging from a leaf the size of a small coin to 14–15in (35–38cm) across. Some have small, silky hairs, giving the leaf a soft, flannelly feel, while sometimes they are sticky to the touch. Shapes may be simple and round, or cut and divided to such an extent that the leaf looks more like a carrot top. Green is the most common leaf colour, but fine hairs give a grey appearance, and dark markings add to the wide colour range. Flowers range from white, pink, salmon, red, cream and mauve to nearly black, and as already mentioned, some are night-scented. Blooms are sized from the tiniest imaginable to over 2in (5cm) across. There are normally five petals, however in some species only two or four are visible. In all cases, the species will have two upper petals, usually the largest, with three or less lower petals. In the wild some species have become crossed, creating what are known as Primary Hybrids, but this is a fairly rare occurrence; occasionally man has developed new hybrids too but this is even more rare.

Pelargoniums are mentioned in old apothecary manuals and have been used to soothe sore throats. Diarrhoea and dysentery were evidently relieved by a potion made from the leaves and roots. Today the foliage of some Scented-leaved forms are used as an infusion to condition the hair and freshen the skin. There is a high quality

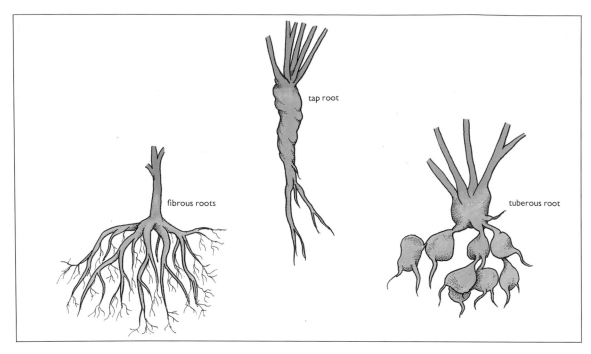

Fig 5 The three types of root formations.

Fig 6 P.bowkeri illustrating the diverse foliage shapes in the family. The blooms are light purplish and the petals are fringed.

oil present in the leaves, stem and stalk, which may be extracted. With the growing popularity in the use of herbs, the *Pelargonium* has found a niche in the kitchen and is also used as a basis for pot-pourri. The bright red petals will stain the skin when rubbed on to it and women in some cultures have used these petals as a skin paint and to dye fabrics.

It is not usual to find extensive collections of *Pelargonium* species in private greenhouses, but there are some enthusiasts who value this part of the fancy. These plants are not grown commercially on a large scale and even then are only offered by specialist nurseries. It is possible to acquire seeds, often through the seed distribution schemes of specialist societies, or as a gift from a *Pelargonium* species grower.

The following list will give the reader an idea of the vast and varied forms and colours of these fascinating plants. However, they generally do require a little more attention than the cultivars.

Fig 7 P.odoratissimum *is a small-growing apple-scented species, useful in pot-pourri and in cookery. It seeds readily and is easy to grow and propagate, either by cuttings or from seed.*

## SPECIES LIST

One or two examples from each section have been listed, together with their basic requirements. However, it must be remembered that these notes are to be used only as a guide, because many plants will try to do their best in the British climate, often at very different times and formations from their wild, natural growing programme. Any species normally grown for their aromatic foliage are included in the Scented-leaved plant list on pages 112–113.

## Section *Hoarea*

The group usually has a single tuber as a root. They are dormant in early autumn and winter, beginning to grow foliage in late winter or early spring and blooming soon after. *Hoarea* types are a little difficult to propagate; choose July or August. They have beautiful blooms of five petals.

**P.barklyi**   A geophyte, with roundish foliage, very recessed veins and an attractive narrow zone on the dark green, hairy leaves which are red to purple underneath. The blooms are pale cream on long, reddish and hairy stems. A small-growing plant that will not get out of hand. Use a well-drained, light compost mixture and keep dry when dormant, water sparingly at other times. It grows often in rocky, south-facing slopes. Propagate the plant by seed or by removing tubers when more than one is present.

**P.incrassatum**   A geophyte with small tubers. Quite large flower heads containing up to twenty-five magenta blooms. Often in flower before the leaves have fully erupted. Foliage is covered with silky hairs and is of a feather shape with the lobes irregularly cut. It is about 10in (25cm) high, while in bloom. Propagate by tubers or by seed. Do not water the plant while it is dormant. Water it sparingly when growth begins in late winter. *P.incrassatum* grows on stony ground in the wild.

## Section *Seymouria*

*Seymouria* very similar to *Hoarea*. The blooms have two petals only. A difficult section to grow.

**P.asarifolium**   Meaning Asarum-leaved. A geophyte with small, elongated tubers. The leaves have no stalk, and are silver-grey beneath, due to the presence of short, thickly-growing hairs. The upper leaves are shiny and green, and roundish in shape. The blooms are small and narrow with dark red to purplish petals. The plant grows in stony sand or clay-loam areas and is very rare.

## Section *Polyactium*

They usually have underground tubers and some in this group are of a succulent habit. The five petalled flowers are star-like, and are often night-scented. *Pelargonium triste* belongs to this section.

**P.fulgidum**   This plant has a semi-succulent stem and heart-shaped leaves, lobed and divided, and covered with fine hairs which give a silky appearance to this low-growing, shrubby plant. Blooms are bright scarlet. *P. fulgidum* has been used as parent to a number of hybrids. It grows in rocky, windy areas and on coastland.

**P.caffrum**   This geophyte has a large underground tuber sometimes rising above soil level. The five petals are finely divided giving a feathery look to the largish blooms which are dark purple or sometimes of a lighter hue. The foliage is deeply and complicatedly dissected. An even temperature is needed and it will enjoy plenty of water in the growing season as long as the compost is well drained. In the wild, *P.caffrum* grows mainly in grasslands in Southern Africa which are often burnt during high summer. Propagate this plant from seed or tubers but, as it is rare in cultivation, it is wise to be cautious when dividing tubers.

## Section *Otida*

These are succulents with fleshy leaves and fairly small flowers.

**P.alternans**   This smallish plant grows in the dry western and south-western Cape areas, often among rocky places not far from the coast. A mature plant will resemble a small, old tree. Dark brown bark covers the succulent stems and trunk. The leaves look like the top of

Fig 8 P.caffrum, a plant for the real enthusiast. It has an underground tuber from which large segmented leaves rise. In the wild it grows mainly in the eastern Cape Province of Southern Africa.

a carrot and are grey-green. The five-petalled white to pink flowers set seed quite readily. They may be grown from cuttings or by seed. Water the plant very sparingly and give it plenty of light.

**P.carnosum** This plant has a thick, smooth stem often without the grey-green, much-cut leaves. The flowers are small, whitish and have five petals. It is easy to grow in a soil-based compost with a good helping of grit. However, you must be careful not to overwater it, or it will die.

## Section *Ligularia*

The plants in this section have woody-based succulent stems and carrot-like foliage. The flowers have five petals.

**P.crassipes** Often un-branched with persistent, dry petioles, the stems of this plant are short. The foliage is much cut and light green in colour. The blooms are smallish and can be from salmon-pink through to mauve with darker veining. Water it sparingly and pot into well-drained compost with added grit.

**P.ionidiflorum** Of small proportions, when the wiry stem of this plant becomes mature it is covered with bark. The leaves are oval, lobed and cut deeply. The violet-magenta flowers comprise five narrow petals. It grows on rocky slopes, so use a gritty loam-based compost. Keep watering to a minimum, but increase it when the plant is in full bloom. *P.ionidiflorum* grows well from seed or cutting material.

## Section *Jenkinsonia*

A small section of half-shrubs or succulents. The blooms may have five or four petals, depending on the species.

**P.endlicherianum** A herbaceous perennial that is one of the exceptions to the rule regarding hardiness. *P.endlicherianum* is hardy during mild winters in Britain. In fact, it does not like greenhouse conditions in our winter, which can make the plant difficult to grow or bloom, due to most growers being nervous of allowing it an outdoor winter existence. I have a 4-year-old plant grown in tufa rock, in a rockery situation outdoors. The many leaves are set in a rosette fashion from the corky root-stock, often above the surface. The flowers have five petals with the upper two being the larger, the blooms are a light magenta with carmine markings, and sometimes scented. It is best to propagate it from seed and it is more likely to be hardy from British-grown plants.

**P.tetragonum** With a square stem on a succulent, sprawling plant, *P.tetragonum* is good to use as an unusual hanging pot plant. The blooms are large and can be pink or cream and there are only four petals with the upper ones being much larger. It is easy to grow, but remember to withhold copious watering in winter and give it plenty while it is in bloom. Leaves are almost ivy-shaped and have a red edge to the grey, hairy foliage. Propagate the plant from stems broken at a node and planted in sand.

*Fig 9* P.tetragonum, *an easy-to-grow species for the beginner to try. The plant has square, trailing stems, small leaves and flowers that may be pink or cream in varying shades. It is a true succulent.*

## Section *Myrrhidium*

Some are annuals, some half-shrubs. Four or five petals may be found.

**P.canariense (synonym P.candicans)** This plant has long, straggly, thin branches. The leaves are a long heart shape, lobed and with crenations. The leaves are covered in thin silky hairs and are green with a grey tone. The two upper petals are larger, and the flowers are white to pale pink. It is easy to grow, but not often available.

**P.urbanum** This is another sprawling half-shrub with well-cut lobed foliage. The blooms are very attractive due to the top two petals being so much larger. They can be either pink or deep cream with dark red markings. Its natural habitat is sandy, coastal scrubland.

## Section *Peristera*

Most of the plants in this section are annuals, or possibly short-lived perennials in British greenhouses.

**P.australe**  This plant is not always short lived, but does not have longevity. It is very variable in height from a few inches to 3ft (1m). The leaves are in proportion and heart-shaped with a rounded tip, they are soft and covered in hairs. Some varieties of this species have many short hairs. The foliage has a strange, fairly unpleasant odour. *P.australe* is very rampant, especially the larger forms. The smallish blooms are mauve to violet with darker blotchings and veinings. The smaller forms are most attractive, but the larger forms need space equivalent to

*Fig 10 P.canariense synonym P.candicans, a small-growing species with large flowers.*

their size. Cuttings and seeds are easy. The plant comes from around Australia and New Zealand.

**P.iocastrum**  A charming species, it could be described as a miniature version of *P.australe* without its vigorous habit. It does not like to be overwatered nor dried out and will tolerate light shade as well as sun.

## Section *Camphylia*

Small, short plants with oval leaves.

**P.elegans**  The foliage is tough for such a special species, more rounded than others in this section and has a reddish edging to the serrated margin. The flowers have five large petals of delicate pink with purple marks on the top two petals. It grows in sand dunes and other sandy areas. The roots are stoloniferous and can be used for propagating; seed if available, is the other method, as cuttings are difficult to root.

**P.violareum**  This is sometimes known by the synonyms *P.tricolor* and *P.holosericeum*. The name '*violareum*', viola, is most apt for the shape and appearance of the bloom, its colour is whitish to palest mauve with large light magenta blotches on the two upper petals, which also possess raised, near-black markings at their base. The foliage is a long oval with serrations, and is grey-green due to the fine, soft hairs. The plant grows in sandy soils and is short with short branches, the total height being about 10–12in (25–30cm).

## Section *Dibrachya*

This section is the ancestor of the Ivy-leaved type, with slender, sprawling stems and ivy-shaped foliage.

**P.peltatum**  The ancestor of the Ivy-leaved type cultivars. It has thin, brittle stems and stalks

15

and is of a scrambling or climbing habit. The leaves are ivy-shaped and have a dark zone in the centre. Flowers are large and mauve, *P.peltatum* is easy to grow and the cuttings root well.

**P.saxafragoides** Almost a miniature species. The wiry branches and stems are slender but short noded. The leaves are also ivy-shaped and aromatic when crushed. The blooms are small and mauve with dark purple lines.

## Section *Eumorpha*

These are shrubby, herbaceous plants with slender stems. The top petals are broad, the leaves palmate and lobed, on long petioles.

**P.alchemilliodes** A slender, scrambling species, sometimes with zoned leaves softly covered in hairs, like the stems and leaf stalks. The blooms are five-petalled and usually salmon to pink, but sometimes cream. Propagation should not be a problem with any of the plants in this section, as the seed is set with all of them. *P.alchemilliodes* is easy to grow; in the wild it inhabits rocky slopes and hilltop crevices.

**P.grandiflorum** When crushed, the smooth leaves are freshly aromatic, they are grey-greenish, usually with a strong zone. The plant tends to straggle in a greenhouse, but in the wild is erect and herbaceous. The large flowers are pink to mauve, the two upper petals larger and darker with markings and veining, probably used in raising some cultivars. Found in the mountains, *P.grandiflorum* is quite easy to keep, and strikes well from cuttings and germinates well from seed.

## Section *Glaucophyllum*

The plants in this section have fleshy, simple leaves without much lobing, some are well cut, usually grey. They are small plants with woody mature stems and grey-green leaves.

**P.glaucum** It has long, pointed, grey foliage and is thick and succulent-like with entire margins to the leaves. The blooms are creamy-yellow and have red markings on the top petals. The plant has a small stature and grows in rocky and sandy places. Do not overwater it. Cuttings can be troublesome, seed would be more successful.

**P.ternatum** A shrublet growing in exposed areas, of which some could be exposed to slight frosts. There are three lobes to the rough, greenish leaves. It is sturdy and upright in growth and will need pinching out to keep under control. The blooms are pale pinkish-mauve with darker striations in the top petals. It is easy to take cuttings from semi-ripe or young stems.

## Section *Ciconium*

One of the main sections to supply ancestors to the Zonal cultivars. These are half-shrubs or shrubs with thick, fleshy stems. The leaves are largely rounded heart- or kidney-shaped, some with noticeable leaf zonation.

**P.inquinans** This plant has soft, velvety mid-green leaves without a strong zone. The bloom consists of five petals of bright scarlet, the petals being almost the same size. Tall specimens can reach 3ft (1m). It is very easy to grow and propagate from stem cuttings. Water it well while blooming, but gradually reduce watering as winter approaches.

**P.monstrum** An unusual plant that can sometimes be difficult to acquire, even from the specialist. The foliage is round- to heart-shaped and very shiny. The margins of the leaves are very crisp and curled, with a faint zone visible. The stems are straight and short noded with persistent stipules. *P.monstrum* rarely flowers in 'captivity', however, the blooms comprise five light magenta petals with some slight veining. It is not tall growing and

Fig 11 Pelargonium inquinans, *a species type of the Ciconium section.*

cuttings are difficult to root. The rest of this section is reasonably simple to propagate, so *P.monstrum* is not often persevered with.

## Section *Cortusina*

This section contains plants with short, fleshy stems with the stipules remaining and seeming like spikes. The foliage is reniform, and some plants are woolly.

### P.magentum (synonym P.rhodanthum)
A shrublet without the characteristic persistent stipules. The small leaves are grey-green. Growing on stony, rocky areas, it soon becomes woody. The flowers are large for the size of the plant and are a beautiful magenta with large, darker markings on all petals. It often blooms through the winter in my own collection.

### P.sidoides (synonym P.sidaefolium)
Grows in many types of areas from stony soil, to clay and loam, and in grassland. It has a thick underground root from which the long leaf stalks arise in a crown-like formation. The leaves are soft, grey-green, heart-shaped and somewhat hairy. The small, narrow petals are nearly black in colour. The plant likes plenty of light and not too much water. It is fairly easy to grow from seed, but cuttings may be difficult to obtain because of the rosette formation on the short stems.

## Section *Pelargonium*

Woody, branched shrubs and half-shrubs. Leaves are usually lobed and divided.

### P.cucullatum
The main parent of the Regal types. The leaves are cupped and of a slightly triangular shape with serrations at the margins, often with a reddish line. The flowers are medium to large and pink-purple, or sometimes darker and they have markings and veinings on the two upper petals. A vigorous grower, easy to grow and propagate from cuttings taken from the younger growth.

### P.panduriforme
An erect and branching shrub which may reach well over 3ft (1m) in height. The leaves are somewhat oakleaf-shaped and soft to the touch; they are light green with soft hairs. The flowers are pale pink, the upper two are veined and they fold over each other at times. It is easy to grow and propagate from cuttings, but this species is not often found.

## Section *Isopetalum*

There is only one species in this section and it comes from St Helena, an island in the Atlantic Ocean.

### P.cotyledonis
A succulent stem species of small stature. It has very few rounded, heart-shaped leaves which grow on short leaf-stalks. They are bright green in colour and change to darker green and then red with age, before falling from the plant. The flowers are small, pure white and equal in size. This is a charming

*Fig 12* Pelargonium *x* ardens, *a red-flowered primary hybrid.*

plant, but it is difficult to find cutting material from the few branches which are thick. Try to grow it from seed, if possible. Grow it in well-drained soil and water carefully.

## Primary Hybrids

Hybrids result from genetically dissimilar parents. Offspring from different species were first evident hundreds of years ago and these early crosses are now known as Primary Hybrids of which a few are still available. Most are beautiful specimens and worth growing. Their names are prefixed with an 'x' to show that they are crosses.

***P.x ardens*** This cross has a thick, woody stem with oval, heart-shaped leaves. The flowers are dark scarlet with even darker markings. Raised in London about 1800, it is a cross between *P.lobatum* and *P.fulgidum*.

***P.x glaucifolium*** Thought to be a cross between *P.gibbosum* and *P.lobatum* achieved in the 1820s. It is tall, with nobbly stems of a succulent nature. The leaves are large, grey-green and lobed. The flowers are a very deep purple, nearly black, and the petals are edged with a pencil line of yellow. The flowers are also very scented at night.

***P.x Schottii*** Again *P.lobatum* and *P.fulgidum* feature in this plant's parentage. It has soft, feathery leaves that are quite large. The flowers are purplish to crimson in differing hues.

18

CHAPTER 2

# Scented-leaved Pelargoniums

Many of these wild plants have aromatic foliage and are listed as Scented-leaved Pelargoniums or Scented-leaved 'geraniums'. It is not really certain why the foliage is so aromatic. To humans, most of the aromas are in the main very pleasant, but to grazing animals they are sometimes even poisonous. The leaves produce oil through glandular hairs on the leaves, stalks and stems, which is emitted when the plant is touched. In hot sun, these oils will give off a hazy gas which will protect the plant from extreme glare and heat.

The use of some varieties of Scented Pelargoniums in the perfume industry is an important

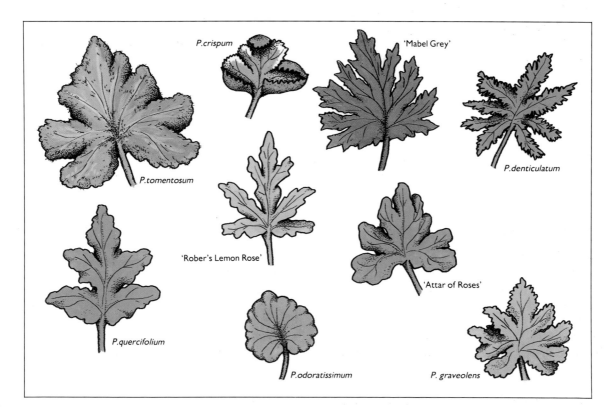

*Fig 13 Some scented species leaf forms.*

economic factor and vast fields of the plants are harvested just before they bloom, and processed as an essential oil. Reunion Island is one of the main producers, using mainly *P.capitatum* and *P.graveolens* which have a strong rose or rose-lemon scent. Geraniol and citronellol are present in all green parts of the plant. As well as rose, which is classed as a flower aroma, there are also fruit, herb and spice scents, as well as what are usually described as aromatic or pungent scents. These latter are not often as pleasant. However, with all these aromas, their strength depends on other factors. Plants grown hot, dry and in full sun will smell different to those grown in shade and watered well. The description of each aroma or scent will vary with an individual's sense of smell and interpretation of the aroma, but the overall effect is fairly universal.

Most of the scented plants derived initially from the *Ligularia, Pelargonium* and *Cortusina* sections and are of a sub-shrub habit often with a tendency to sprawl, although there are some with a nice compact habit and some which will grow to enormous proportions. The foliage varies in size, shape and colour as well as scent. The size of the blooms on most varieties can only be described as small to medium and, although some modern hybrids are larger, it must be said that these plants are really grown for the scented foliage and the blooms are an added attraction. It is pleasing to see that many nurseries and garden centres are now selling at least the more common and popular varieties.

Fig 14 'Golden Clorinda.' This large-flowered scented variety has a lovely golden edge to its leaves.

If you are looking for a more unusual variety, then it is best to buy your plants from a specialist nursery. In the following list the scents and habits of Scented-leaved Pelargoniums are recorded.

## UNIQUE PELARGONIUMS

It is generally accepted, and indeed in part correct, that the origin of Uniques is the lovely *Pelargonium* species *P.fulgidum*. *P.fulgidum* has bright scarlet blooms, quite small felty leaves and is a succulent. *P.fulgidum* is also responsible for a few more cultivars, introducing the scarlet colour. Other species were used in the breeding of Uniques and it is apparent that *P.cucullatum* introduced the mauve colour to the flowers, and perhaps *P.betulinum* could account for the white-flowered form. It is almost certain that they have also been crossed with Regals somewhere along the way. The colours of the blooms are white, pink, salmon, scarlet, crimson, mauve, magenta through to purple, while some are flecked and veined and have darker or contrasting markings which are more pronounced on the upper two of the five petals. In shape, the single blooms are similar to Regals but slightly smaller, and there are not many blooms to the head of flowers — from three to eight is average. The foliage is quite large and strong, and a deep green colour, lobed into five sections with teeth or crenations. Often Uniques are very aromatic. The plants themselves are very shrubby and tend to become woody, so will require cutting back or light pruning from time to time, but care must be taken that this is not undertaken three months before the natural flowering season, which is in early summer, because they will form flower buds on the ends of younger growth. A few are fairly compact but most can grow up to 4ft (1.25m) or more.

About 150 years ago Uniques were introduced as a garden bedding type, there were many listed and of many colour combinations.

Fig 15 'Shrubland Pet Unique', showing a reversion of the blooms.

Unfortunately today there remain only a handful of what we term Uniques. Research reveals a problem, in that the early plants do not seem to be of the same type as today's Unique and where records failed is not clear. It is known that Uniques currently recognised were popular in Victorian times, but many of the varieties grown then have long since disappeared.

It is best to grow them as pot plants and, given ideal conditions, some varieties will soon reach the roof of a conservatory or greenhouse. In summer months Uniques look attractive in large patio pots or as a backdrop in the herb garden; their unusual flower colour and scented leaves are a pleasant addition.

CHAPTER 3

# Regal Pelargoniums

Other names for this group include 'Martha Washington', 'Lady Washington' as they are known in America, 'Show Pelargoniums' and in earlier times 'Grandiflorums'. The scientific title for Regals used by botanists is *Pelargonium x domesticum (Bailey)* which was given to Regals by the botanist L H Bailey, but the Bailey is now usually dropped and *Pelargonium x domesticum* accepted.

Regals have been in cultivation for centuries. Serious hybridising has taken place in France and Germany as well as in England, since before 1900. The species used in this breeding were, it is thought, *P.anglosum*, *P.cucullatum*, *P.fulgidum* and *P.grandiflorum*. It is possible that more species were 'dipped into' to create the wonderful, showy plant of today.

The suitability of the Regal as a house plant, show plant and collectors' plant is unquestionable. The fact that the Regal lends itself to forcing into bloom earlier than other types of cultivars makes it a popular money-spinner in the horticultural trade with Easter and Mother's Day celebrations occurring in the spring. Its usual time of showing the first good flush of flower is in May and June. Subsequent flowering is never as prolific until the following year. The very colourful blooms are medium to large, with soft reds, pink, salmon, orange, mauve, purple, darkest maroon and white. Veining is normally evident in varying amounts, as is flecking and blotching either in darker or contrasting hues and there are central marks usually of a deep purple or maroon on the upper two petals. In some varieties, more than one colour makes up the overall effect, even with pencil lines at the outer edges of each petal. A few double or semi-double forms exist, but most have five petals. The shape of each bloom is often referred to as Petunia- or Azalea-shaped, which is a fair description although frilled, fringed or ruffled effects may be found. The older, established varieties have this formation of two upper petals and three lower ones. The flower head can contain as

*Fig 16 Regal foliage and bloom.*

Regal          Zonal          Ivy-leaved

*Fig 17 Basic* Pelargonium *foliage shapes.*

many as fifteen individual flowers or florets each perhaps 2–3in (5–7cm) across.

All Regals have the same or very nearly the same shaped foliage, which is normally stiff and covered with short hairs that can only be seen close to. If a leaf was opened out it would have a lobed, triangular shape with much serration and its natural tendency to be cup-shaped may be only a slight concave or to such an amount that the leaf would hold water. They are mid- to darkish green in colour with a greyish tone when the hairs are long. There are some, although not many, variegated forms of Regals.

This shrubby plant soon becomes barky and woody in all but young growth. On the stems stipules are evident in pairs where the leaf stalk (petiole) joins the stem. Regals are somewhat straggly in habit, at least in the older varieties.

Modern varieties are being developed to be naturally branching as well as producing more than one good flush of blooms. These ensure a rounded bushy specimen, but taller growing Regals will reach 3ft (1m) or more in a couple of years. The roots are fibrous, often developing a stoloniferous nature, enabling young plants to be produced from the roots – it is possible to propagate Regals from root cuttings (*see* page 76). It is pretty certain that most greenhouse or house plant growers will have had a Regal Pelargonium at some time. Nurseries, garden centres and even supermarkets find them a subject of quick turnover, but only the few popular varieties are offered. Less common varieties will be readily available from your usual supplier of special pelargoniums.

## ANGELS, DWARFS AND MINIATURE REGALS

The Regal category also contains Angels, Dwarf and Miniature Regals. To the surprise of some, these are not technically the same, but thanks to recent publications, Angels are being understood in their own right. They have a doubtful past. In the early 1800s a form appeared which was similar to a Regal, but much more compact; no one seems to know its actual origin apart from the possibility of it being derived from *P.dumosum* (itself not known today). Today, as far as is certain, 'Angeline' (as it was known) has disappeared from catalogues and collections. However, because of the lack of evidence and no stronger argument against, it must be assumed that our Angels are the result of a re-introduction of the 'Angeline' line. Other plants were used in this hybridising; *Pelargonium*

*crispum* being a major factor. Mr Arthur Langley Smith, a London school teacher, was a great hybridiser of the Angels – he began his work in the early 1900s. He is known as 'The Father of the Angels' and his popular Angel 'Catford Belle' was introduced in 1935. It is still going strong and is a favourite with all who grow Angels.

The plants are of a shorter stature than the Regal with an annoying habit of becoming straggly if not pruned or pinched out. The stems are quite thin and brittle in immature growth, later becoming woody and covered with thin brownish bark like the Regal. The foliage is mid-green and generally ½in–1in (1–2.5cm), rather crisp and ruffled, due to the evidence of *P.crispum* in its ancestry. *P.crispum* is also responsible for the fact that some have delicately scented leaves.

In America, Angels are often known as

*Fig 18 An Angel from America, 'Seely's Pansy'.*

*Fig 19 Bedding design using 'Tip Top Duet'. Angels are useful and long-lasting plants for outdoor work.*

'Pansy-faced Pelargoniums' – a very apt description of the flower because the petals *do* overlap somewhat and most also possess large purple markings on the two top petals. The size of the bloom is variable from ½in–1in (1–4cm). The main colour is mauve to purple with white, and a touch of maroon in some varieties. The blooms may be a little on the small side, but their quantity and the fact that they flower far longer than Regals and do not dislike outdoor life, more than compensates. Not only are they good for tubs, beds and so on, Angels also adapt to growing indoors more readily than many *Pelargonium* forms and their smaller habit ensures a tidy pot plant for the window-sill.

It is a pity that Angels are not easy to come by from general nurseries or garden centres. However, they have become so popular over recent years that it won't be long before it is not only the specialists who stock them.

The terms 'miniature' and 'dwarf' Regals are somewhat misleading, for neither are dwarf or miniature in the true pelargonium sense of the word, and only two are reputed to be actual miniature sports of Regals. So it is far safer to refer to all of this type as Angels and, if exhibiting, they would all be classified together. The 'miniature' Regals available have blooms that are soft mauve with the two top petals entirely marked with a darker purple that has dark red overtones. The foliage of these plants is not so stiff and shiny as the Angel and is not scented.

CHAPTER 4

# Zonal Pelargoniums

Zonal Pelargoniums are widely known as 'geraniums', *Pelargonium x hortorum (Bailey)* or *P.x. hortorum* for the real expert. Quite a few pelargonium species form part of their make-up, the most important ancestors being *P.inquinans* and *P.zonale*, both of which come from the *Ciconium* section of the species. Others used over the years include *P.frutetorum* and *P.alchemilliodes* which are also important origins of the Zonal. In fact, there may be other species that have been introuced into this form to a lesser degree.

The first Zonal seen in England was recorded by Dillenius, in the 1730s, but it is presumed to have been introduced hundreds of years previously. The name 'Zonal' is a little misleading, because not all Zonal Pelargoniums have a visible horseshoe zone of a darker tone on their foliage, which is what gives them the name, as well as the common name of Horseshoe Pelargonium (or Horseshoe 'geranium'). This zoning feature shows their strong link with the species *P.zonale*. Some varieties have this dark marking in the centre of the leaf

single of a primitive form

single

semi-double

double

typical Regal bloom

*Fig 20 Four Basic Zonal Pelargonium blooms in contrast to a Regal bloom (right).*

and this would signify that the plant had *P. frutetorum* as a parent somewhere along the line.

Since those early days of hybridising so many forms have been developed that sub-groupings have been established with subtitles that describe the various forms and habits — Rosebud-flowered, Cactus-flowered and Fancy-leaved, now known as Ornamental Foliage Varieties. Stellar types have both unusual foliage and flowers, including a form known commonly as the Five-fingered Hybrids which has narrow ragged petals, and many Fiat forms which have serrated petals. These sub-groups also include Miniature, Dwarf and a classification termed 'unclassified', which contains those not fitting neatly into any of the classifications, and these complete the vast range. Zonals have also been crossed with the Ivy-leaved types (*see* page 45).

Zonal blooms may be single, with five petals, semi-double, with six to eight petals, or double, with the number of petals exceeding eight. Flower size is very variable, from the primitive shape and size of its single form (with the top two petals being separated from the lower three), to the mammoth-sized rounded blooms with petals overlapping, which have been developed over the centuries. Some miniature-growing varieties have individual flowers of only ¼in (6mm) and in the larger-flowering forms perhaps 3in (7–8cm) across. The colour range is endless from white (very occasionally cream), pink, red, coral, orange, salmon, mauve to magenta in lots of hues and mixes. The blooms often have outlines or splashing of another shade, and veining on some or all of the petals with blotching, usually towards the centre of the bloom, known as the 'eye' in descriptive lists. Zonal Pelargoniums are in every basic colour imaginable, except true blue. Basic Zonals may have over 100 pips (florets) to each flower head (umbel). The normal growing single, semi-double and double flowering forms are known as 'Basic Zonals' to distinguish them from the Miniatures, Ornamental types and so on.

The plants in this section usually have rounded heart-shaped leaves with shallow lobes and some rounded teeth at the margins. They are mainly soft in texture, with hairs covering the surface. There may be a zone present, either as a wide band or as a thin line nearer to, or at, the margin, or show as a dark blotch in the centre of the leaf. These zones show on the upper surface of the leaf. It is not uncommon to find that the leaves have red undersides. Leaves are often mid to dark green, but light green to nearly yellow (known as 'Golden-leaved) and variegated foliage is also common. The size of the foliage depends on the type, but ranges from less than ½in (1cm) in the miniatures to 4in (10cm) across, in the basic Zonals.

The mature Zonal Pelargonium is served by a fairly small fibrous root system, and in young rooted cuttings the roots are white and very brittle. Old established varieties may reach upwards of 6–10ft (1.8–3m), but it is more usual to keep plants to a more manageable size around 2–3ft (60–90cm), in modern situations. If housed in a conservatory or high-roofed greenhouse with adequate light, particularly natural light from above, Zonals will continue to become larger especially if a warmer than usual atmosphere is kept during the winter months. This enables the plant to continue growing; flowering will also continue during the winter, somewhat sparser than in the summer, but nevertheless a welcome sight. If plants are growing in the roof or near to glass, during very sunny spells in midsummer, remember to shade the glass to avoid scorching.

The main stems may become covered in a pale cream to buff, waxy looking soft bark, which will become hard, and if the plant is not cut back to encourage new growth, it will be difficult for new young shoots to break from these semi-woody stems. The immature stems are often brittle and succulent and the stipules thereon will also be green, becoming a light, papery brown with age and desiccating before dropping from the older plant stems.

27

Fig 21 'Halloween', a fully double Zonal with the foliage of the P.filicifolium type.

## 'IRENES'

Both 'Irenes' and 'Fiats' are currently out of favour because they are too large for today's greenhouses and gardens. 'Irenes' were developed after years of work in the USA partly during, and then after, the Second World War. Charles Behringer of Ohio introduced the first of this series in 1942 and named it after his wife 'Irene'. After this, other breeders used 'Irene' to create more of these strong, fast-growing, large plants with large, mid-green, soft foliage, sometimes heavily zoned and with 'blousey' flowers. Hartsook and Bode, both Americans, worked during the 1960s with French strains to enhance the large semi-double blooms. It is possible that some of the 'Irene' varieties were sports from other varieties in the range. 'Irenes' are so large and vigorous that adult plants need a great deal of growing space and cannot sit on an ordinary-sized window-sill; a large greenhouse area or similar is required. Careful feeding is also required as too much nitrogen will encourage the foliage to become large and soft at the expense of the blooms. Blooms come in a variety of colours including red, salmon, and blue-red and two white varieties which are medium sized. Outdoor work with 'Irenes' in a damp British summer may be problematical, due to too much water and too little light, encouraging a soft growth habit which makes the plant susceptible to fungal problems. Too rich a soil, both in the open ground and in the pot, will discourage flowering. The blooms are held on long stems which make them ideal for cutting and they will last for weeks as a lovely display in water.

## 'FIATS'

'Fiats' were first raised in France in about 1870 by Paul Bruant. Another strain of strong, vigorous self-branching plants, 'Fiats' have a soft green foliage that has very little or no zone and large heads of blooms on strong stems, showing off the good-sized semi-double or double florets. The colours soft orange and salmon-pink dominate and a few varieties have attractive, serrated petals. Somewhat shorter and more self-branching than 'Irenes', many varieties today have 'Fiats' in their ancestry, including some of the 'Irenes'. Because of the soft, large foliage and the stocky growth, there is a chance of fungal diseases in the centre of the plant – a careful eye on this type of situation is recommended, especially if the plants are housed out of doors or in a cool place. Once again, due to the 'Fiats' growth rate and habit, these types have fallen out of favour with most growers and gardeners, which is a shame because given adequate care they will prove to be very eye-catching, not least because some varieties have attractive, serrated edges to the petals with veining and shading to the petals.

## 'DEACONS'

This is one of the most modern of all the sections or types. The first 'Deacon' was introduced in 1970 at the Chelsea Flower Show by Wick Hill Geraniums (which is no longer in business). This section is due to many years of hybridising by the Reverend Stanley Stringer of Suffolk, England who initially cross-bred a Miniature and an Ivy-leaved Pelargonium, then selectively hybridised the offspring. The eighteen that were introduced in the following ten years or so were of a very compact and floriferous habit – in fact living up to the other name sometimes used for this section, Florabunda Pelargonium. Until his death in 1986, Canon Stringer developed and introduced twenty-four 'Deacon' types.

Some of the latter introductions are not quite so compact and self-branching. The leaves are medium-sized and a mid to dark green colour, which is only slightly lobed. Not all have zoning and when zoning is present it will vary in depth and tone – one variety shows a variegation in the centre of the leaf, and there are a few varieties, recently introduced, with golden-green foliage. Blooms are of a semi-double formation, with many florets on each spherical head and many heads to each plant lasting for a long time both in terms of the individual flowers and the overall flowering period. In fact, many 'Deacon' varieties will offer blooms all through the year when warmth and light levels are suitable. Flower colour ranges from white to shades of pink, red, coral and soft orange. Having this naturally compact habit is a real bonus for today's collection, but 'Deacons' will grow into quite large plants given enough root and growing space. The heads will last well in water and are best used in groups of three or five in an arrangement, due to their ball shape

Fig 22 'Deacon Fireball'.

and size giving a sense of volume when massed in a vase.

'Deacons' are becoming more popular with general gardeners, so garden centres and non-specialist nurseries are at last stocking them, but unfortunately, only a handful of the varieties are available from other than specialist sources, which is a great pity. Another problem with the popular gardening outlet is that the 'Deacons' on sale often do not have the prefix 'Deacon' and are just labelled by the second part of their variety name.

## 'BIRD'S EGG' VARIETIES

The title is apt, describing not the shape of the petals, but the darker spotting on each one, which is sometimes denser nearer the base of

*Fig 23 'Plenty', a basic Zonal with Bird's Egg markings.*

the petal, giving a deeper colour at the centre of the individual bloom. The colour of the spotting or flecking is of a much deeper hue than the petal colour.

Generally, 'Bird's Egg' varieties' growth is medium to leggy, they have small to medium-sized, light green leaves with little or no zone. There is also a golden 'Bird's Egg' variety with very light, yellow-green leaves. Florets may be single or double, of pastel shades or pink or mauve. They originated in the late nineteenth century, coming from France.

More recently, some varieties have been raised with soft, fine, vertical markings of varying densities in the petals, even to some petals having the plain base shade and some having totally the overlaying shade. These markings are mainly on a light base petal colour with the markings being a contrasting or darker colour. The original types were classed as 'Eggshell' varieties, but are often now classed with the 'Bird's Egg' section, quite wrongly. Both these variations of Zonals are found in miniature and dwarf forms. It is unlikely that they will be found in local garden centres, but specialist nurseries will catalogue them.

## 'CACTUS-FLOWERED' VARIETIES

It may be that the term 'Poinsettia-flowered' is used more widely in some countries for the 'Cactus-flowered' variety. The petals are curled vertically or furled and quilled along the length of the petal in a convex fashion, so that the petals appear very narrow. There are single, semi-double and double flowered forms in this section. The blooms can be white, pink, coral, scarlet, crimson or magenta, sometimes with toning stripes or flecks. Each floret is small- to medium-sized with no more than eighteen to twenty blooms on the head, but usually less. The long-stemmed heads are good for cutting and the single forms do not drop readily. Leaves are mid-green with hardly any evidence

bird's egg

carnation-flowered or serrated

cactus or poinsettia

rose bud

single form of stellar

double form of stellar

Figs 24 and 25 Unusual varieties of Zonal blooms.

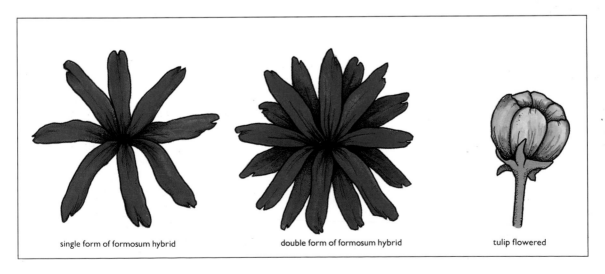

single form of formosum hybrid

double form of formosum hybrid

tulip flowered

of zoning and there is an attractive, silver variegated form which does not seem too robust, but is very desirable. Growth is somewhat straggly so the pinching out of growing tips is recommended. These 'Cactus' varieties were thought to be first introduced in the late 1800s from France and England and now even the miniature and dwarf sections can boast a few varieties. The 'Cactus' varieties will only be found in specialist catalogues.

## 'ROSEBUD-FLOWERED' VARIETIES

'Rosebuds' or 'Noisettes' have been giving pleasure for over a hundred years, and it is a pity that there are so few in cultivation today, compared to those in the past. They are called 'Rosebuds' because of their resemblance to the bud formation of that popular flower. There are many petals in each bud, lying in such a tight and flat manner that it is impossible for them all to open fully, giving a tight rosebud effect to the mature bloom. Individually, the flowers are small- to medium-sized, and are pink or white tipped pink, red, scarlet, magenta or near purple. Some varieties possess petals of a paler base colour, and when you look at the reverse, an attractive colour scheme is visible. Because of the tight florets, it is advisable to use 'Rosebud' types for indoor work. The flower heads contain about eight to twelve blooms, which, being set on long stems, are suitable for

*Fig 26 'White Birds Egg'.*

flower arranging. The leaves are small to medium in size and a mid-green colour with little zonation. The natural growth is inclined to be weak and straggly, so pinching out is necessary at the first potting-up stage. The miniature and dwarf sections have one or two 'Rosebud' varieties. A specialist nursery would supply these types, although 'Apple Blossom Rosebud' is such a favourite that, within the past five years, general nurseries and garden centres have begun to have it on sale.

## 'STELLARS'

This section also has other names by which it is known both in the UK and throughout the world. 'Stellars' originated in Australia from Mr Ted Both of Sydney and were called 'Both's Staphs' or 'Staphs' because it is believed that the species *P.staphysagroides* was crossed with *P.hortorum* to give the start to the breeding of thirty or more 'Stellars'. It is the foliage shape of pointed lobes which gives rise to the name 'Stellar', meaning star. The leaves usually have some zone, and in most varieties the zone is very heavy. There is a variety which has a central dark mahogany blotch as a zone and one or two varieties with yellow-green foliage and dark zones. They were first introduced to Europe in 1966 and have proved to be popular with enthusiasts, but not so much with general growers. The florets consist of pointed, forked upper petals and variably wedge-shaped lower ones. The blooms are medium to large, and usually there are from eight to twenty florets on each truss or head. Colours range through white to pink, orange, red and purple, often with shading and flecking. There are single or double as well as miniature and dwarf forms. A form known as 'Startel' was developed by a seed company a few years ago and a strain of large-flowering forms has come from a nursery in Germany – these latter can be seen at garden centres, while the remainder are found in catalogues or from specialist growers.

## 'FIVE FINGERED', 'FINGERED FLOWERED' OR 'FORMOSUM' AND 'FORMOSA' HYBRID VARIETIES

A little similar in flower and leaf pattern, but not off-shoots to 'Stellars'. The story of this *Pelargonium* began in the court-yard of a Mexican hotel, when the American Milton Arndt found a small plant and named it 'Formosum' because it was assumed that the plant had found its way via a Japanese sea-going vessel. However, this was later found not to be the case, and another American, a Mr Holmes Miller, thought that to call this little stray 'Fingered Flowered' was a safer move, not only because of its doubtful Eastern origins, but because there was already a different plant by this same name. So the four names for this plant are accepted for the individual plant and the type hybrids. 'Formosum' was first catalogued in about 1964. It is a strange uncompromising type, from which only a handful of varieties have been introduced to date, and these only over the last few years. The foliage has the similar star shape, but is more deeply lobed and cut, while the leaves are small and soft green with a sometimes quite heavy zone. Its general stature tends to be tallish and upright, but the hybrids are smaller, more compact and dense, which gives rise to fungal problems. The flower formation varies slightly in each variety. 'Formosum' has narrow, pointed petals which are situated in a circle around the centre in a shallow cup-shape, others have a vaguely typical pelargonium formation, whether semi-double or double flowered. The colour of the original is coral, while later varieties are salmon or red, sometimes with veinings or white tips to the petals.

## 'TULIP-FLOWERED' VARIETIES

This is another very new type, introduced into Britain and Europe during the early 1980s,

Fig 27 The Tulip-flowered variety, 'Patricia Andrea', showing part of the flower head reverting.

## 'MISCELLANEOUS' VARIETIES

The 'Miscellaneous' varieties are not just a group of odds and ends to be treated as substandard types and varieties; in fact it is just the opposite, because many have unusual foliage, fancy blooms, or are derived from an unknown source, even from uncertain parentage so that they cannot be slotted neatly into the other categories. Some cultivars are so closely related to the species that they are almost primary hybrids; *P.frutetorum* has given us many such varieties. Most do take an example of the primitive flower formation from the species, but a few have double blooms and very attractive foliage. Generally known as 'Frutetorum Hybrids', they have dark green leaves to nearly black, glossy leaves with a pronounced zone and there are also ornamental-leaved forms. Its habit is long and scrambling which is not always an asset in other groups, but here it is a useful plus as it is also fast growing. These varieties are good for baskets, tubs, window-boxes and summer ground cover in the garden, and can be used on large rockeries. The flowers range from a light to a very deep coral, most often on long wiry stems holding the blooms high above the foliage.

In 1930 a seedling was discovered and described at Kew in London and was thus named 'Kewense'. Being so unusual with narrow currant-red petals arranged in the floret as a primitive single, so obviously a straight species-derived plant, it was soon introduced to the nurseries. Since then, colour variations of pink, white and scarlet have been introduced from other hybridists. The medium foliage is darkish green with a dark zone and five lobes which are fairly pointed. The habit is quite neat and compact, but not of a tight formation.

Other varieties with primitive blooms which are carried in small heads on short flower stems, have fine zones like a pencil line, and these occur near the leaf edge or actually on the edge. The foliage is just of a medium size and mid to dark green. The plant will grow

which was originally bred in America, and introduced there in 1966. A 'Fiat' type was used in the first cross and, with subsequent back crosses, Ralph and Robert Andrea raised the first of this type. As the name suggests, the flower is tulip-shaped with more than five petals, but generally not exceeding eight. This pelargonium is called Tulip-flowered because the petals only open partially and have a slightly curved shape. There are only two or three varieties of a basic carmine red at present ranging from salmon to deep red with a much paler reverse. The heads contain about twenty and sometimes up to sixty of these very large florets on long and strong stems. One problem is that the blooms will sometimes revert. Reversion occurs when a part of a plant takes on its original form, usually in a more vigorous manner than the hybrid itself, causing the reverting part to take over completely in some cases. With the Tulip-flowered types, the bloom will revert to the bloom of the 'Fiat' variety in its make-up. All reversions, when detected, should be carefully removed. These vigorous plants have large, soft mid-green foliage with very little zoning. Branches and stalks are also strong, but the distance between leaf joints is short, thus creating a stocky plant.

quite tall if not given the correct amount of light and may have difficulty in producing many blooms. If they are planted outside during the summer or given ideal conditions regarding light, they will continue to be stocky, but rarely bloom profusely. The stipules are large for the size of the main stem, always persistent and remaining green, even when the main stem is old. 'Distinction' is a form with Orient-red flowers, and it also has another name which typifies the foliage pattern, 'One in a Ring'. These types are sometimes listed along with Ornamental Foliage sections in catalogues.

Vesuvius is a very old variety not catalogued today, which has sported a variety with medium-sized foliage and blooms. A sport is a shoot growing on an existing plant, which is unlike the original form. The petals of this sport are striped from the edge, down the length in scarlet and white; any single petal may be of one colour, or divided in definite sections of either of these same colours. No two petals are the same, so the name 'Peppermint Stick' is appropriate, although the plant is more likely to be known as 'New Life'. There are both single and double forms and the relevant prefix completes the name. From 'Single New Life' a form has sported called 'Phlox New Life' with whitish petals slightly flushed pink with a deeply-coloured eye to the bloom. Other 'Phlox' types are available from specialists.

## ORNAMENTAL-FOLIAGED PELARGONIUMS

Normally the term ornamental foliage refers to any of the varieties possessing foliage not of a basic green and with or without a typical zone in the accepted and natural position on the leaf. In this classification come those with very light green, golden or yellow leaves known, for the purposes of classification, as Golden-leaved types. Foliage with light green or yellow-green base colour and either golden or light green markings are popular, as are plain green forms

*Fig 28 Placement of zones in pelargoniums.*

35

with a central cream blotch where there is no chlorophyll present in the leaf. These are known as Butterfly-marked due to the shape of the marking on the leaf. These may be zone-free, or they may have a very light zone, or a heavy zone appearing as a deep mahogany colour.

Patterned foliage, often with veining of a contrasting colour, or with heavy markings or zones in the centre of each leaf, can be found in a few varieties. In some varieties the stems also carry unusual markings and colours. Nearly black foliage is available, as well as foliage with a bronze shade, both of these forms usually have definite zones.

The common names of Variegated or Fancy-leaved varieties are also used for those plants showing multi-coloured foliage. These are known as Bi-coloured or Tri-coloured. Parts of

the leaf of the Bi-coloured form are devoid of chlorophyll, showing either cream or silver-white colouration, as well as the basic green. Sometimes a gentle zone may be observed, but it is so light that it does not show through as a colour, and should only overlap the green parts of the leaf. Put simply, Bi-colours have leaves of two distinct colours other than the zone.

Tri-colours have parts of the foliage devoid of chlorophyll also, but with a deep and pro-nounced visible zone, which should overlay two or more of the other distinctive leaf colours. It has to be understood that the zone in any pelargonium is actually a red pigment, and because the leaves are green, it will show as brown in varying densities. So where the zone is apparent in the chlorophyll-free area, it will show up as red, and where it is present in the green area, it will show as brown. There are,

*Fig 29 'Mr Wren', outstandingly attractive, but can be awkward to grow.*

Fig 30 A Miniature with ornamental foliage, 'Variegated Kleine Liebling' synonym 'Variegated Petit Pierre'.

therefore, four basic colours of red, green, cream (or white) and brown (in varying amounts and strengths) in the Tri-colours and it is this overlaying of each of these colours that gives the attractive compilation of rich hues.

'Reverting' is more common with the Fancy-leaved varieties because of natural instability — any plain green shoots must be removed immediately to prevent the plant losing its coloured growth. Sometimes a coloured sport will develop from a Fancy-leaved or from a normal coloured plant. If the sport is to be nurtured, either take it from the plant and use as cutting material, or remove all normal growth from the plant except the part to which the sport is attached and grow the plant with the sport. Remove any new normal growth that might develop, until it is strong enough to have cuttings taken from it. It is common for a sport to die fairly quickly, but on occasions a healthy sport can be reared to maturity. Often, a shoot will appear that is completely chlorophyll-free. It may look quite attractive, but it will soon shrivel and die because it does not contain any energy-producing chlorophyll. These white shoots are called 'angel' or 'ghost' shoots and are a show fault in exhibition classes.

All sections of *Pelargonium* cultivars have some form or other of Ornamental-foliage types in commerce, except F1 and F2. The first Orna-mental Pelargonium was discovered very soon after the introduction of the first *Pelargonium* cultivar, but it was much later when the Victo-rians encouraged different forms of their favourite plant. Peter Grieve was the most important developer of the Ornamental Pelar-gonium. He lived in the mid-1850s at Culford Hall, Bury St Edmunds and he wrote a book about the subject, with many beautiful plates showing the range of this group. It is pleasing that many of his introductions are still grown today.

The advantages of having beautiful leaves all through the year sometimes leads one to forget the flowers. These are single, semi-double and double in all the colours already found in Zonal Pelargoniums, but white flowers are rare. In some varieties, particularly the earliest known ones, the flowers are small, but modern hybri-disers and 'sport watchers' are working hard to correct this. For really dazzling foliage, experts remove all flowering stems so that all the goodness of the plant is used only by the foliage. Fancy-leaved varieties are a little more tender than most basic types, but they can be used outside in pots and bedding schemes during the summer months, and as many are fairly dwarf in habit, they make an attractive edging to a formal summer bedding scheme.

Some *Pelargonium* cultivars have a harmless virus in their system whereby the veins are cream, giving the leaf a net-like appearance. A few varieties of Ivy-leaved forms and, presently, one Zonal variety, are available with this attract-ive veining. For pot culture in the home, conservatory or greenhouse, good light is essential in adequate amounts to enhance the foliage colour, but harsh summer sun will bleach or even singe the leaves.

Finally, in some nurseries these days, plants are being exposed to radiation, often as a general method of securing virus-free stock commercially, which can encourage abnormally coloured growth.

# F1 HYBRID PELARGONIUMS

Firstly it is important to explain the term F1. An F1 seedling is the first generation of two selected and in-bred parents of stable and true-breeding cultivars. The fruits, or seeds, from an F1 are often sterile and in the event of seed being produced, it will not come true to its original in further crossings.

Unfortunately these F1 pelargoniums are widely known as F1 'geraniums' by breeders, seedhouses and the unsuspecting customer, instead of the correct title, *Pelargonium*, or the full name for this section, the Zonal Pelargonium. The other disturbing factor is that seed raisers and marketeers have often chosen names for these F1s that can be recognised as having being in use for decades, for long-established cultivars.

The hybrid 'geranium' story began in the 1950s, and in 1965 a variety called 'Nittany Lion Red' was bred true to type at Pennsylvania State University, in America. 'Nittany Lion', being the breeding line's name, was the breeding breakthrough after many years and much money was poured into the research. The first F1 'geranium' widely marketed was 'Carefree', which was introduced by Pan American Seed in 1967, then 'New Era' followed. 'Carefree' was soon to be joined by different colour breaks and so the famous 'Carefree' strain was the forerunner of many of today's varieties in the F1 range.

In the early 1970s there was a joint venture between seed companies from Holland and

Fig 31 'Pulsar Salmon'.

America who developed the two varieties 'Sprinter' and 'Cherie'. These are perhaps the two most popular varieties from the early days and the best known by the general public in the UK. They were grown in many famous parks and gardens, often replacing the old faithful cultivar 'Gustav Emich', not without some protest at the time. 'Grenadier' was also very popular and used in similar situations. Other European seed organisations joined Holland in this development work – Italy gave us 'Del Greco' and 'Playboy' and from East Germany came the 'Dresdens' and 'Diamond' series. Holland has also introduced the lovely and easy-to-grow 'Pulsar' range and the fully zoned 'Gala' and 'Sundance', as well as the self-branching or self-breaking 'Breakaway'. The latest introduction is a peltatum (Ivy-leaved) type from America called 'Summer Showers'. This variety comes in a wide range of striking colours including white and possesses fairly large blooms of a primitive peltatum form.

Currently, there are no Regals, Angels, true miniatures, very few Fancy-flowered, no Ornamental-foliage types (unless your own plants develop a sport) and no double-flowered forms readily available and there is only one Ivy-leaved type on offer. F1 'geraniums' have not been totally accepted by the pelargonium enthusiast and it is easy to see why. Those promoting the plant or working on the cultivar nomenclature are not helped by the 'pelargonium/geranium' confusion or the re-using of cultivar names for the F1 pelargonium.

It is true to say that F1s are intended to be used as annual plants for bedding, pot and tub work and for suspended displays. Those who love seasonal colour in the garden, greenhouse or on the patio and uniformity in their displays, are the F1's main fans. They choose to buy F1s from their garden centre perhaps as a seedling, a semi-mature, or as a fully mature and blooming plant. Some of these people are going to become avid enthusiasts of the *Pelargonium* and should be encouraged at all costs.

Seed can be rather expensive because of the many years of in-breeding and testing required before a stable form can be produced, but growing F1 pelargoniums from seed can be great fun. However, F1 pelargoniums are prone to an annoying formation of fruit heads, often referred to as 'sputniks' which detracts from the plants' overall attractiveness, although this trait is being bred out as new varieties are produced.

If the plants are being grown for use as annuals, then the problem of keeping the plants through the winter months will be eliminated. Seed should be sown during the latter period of the cold season (in the UK from January until the end of February) with a germinating soil temperature of 23–25°C (72–75°F). The seeds may be left in an airing-cupboard or similar environment with a stable temperature. Take care to check twice daily for signs of germination, which is recognised by a small slit in the seed-case and the evidence of white growth. Remove the seed immediately, gently weaning it to a cooler situation. When the seedlings have germinated, transfer them very carefully to a seed compost. Sow into pots or trays of good quality, seed-raising compost. Usually, germination will be more speedy and more even than with other *Pelargonium* seed, and as a certain amount of resistance to disease has been bred into the strain, as well as there being no virus from plant material, losses at germination time will also be fewer. The cotyledons (the first seedling leaves) will on the whole be larger, therefore making pricking out easier. Hold the seedling carefully by the cotyledon, and prick into pots or trays of compost. It is important that these cotyledons are not damaged during any stage of the plant's growth, as they are the first means of energy transmission to the plant and will dry up and then fall away naturally when the seedling has developed a strong and independent system. Pot on into a good, well-balanced potting medium with a low fertiliser content. It is important to start the seeds off as early in the season as possible and continue the potting up and potting on process regularly, because seed-grown pelargoniums will take longer to come into flower than those produced by cuttings. Often it will take six months and occasionally longer, if light levels are not high enough to encourage flower bud formation. The plants should be in bud in three to four months. Pinching out should not be necessary during the first season with most modern F1s, in fact it will, of course, delay flowering.

The use of dwarfing agents in commercial nurseries encourages uniformity at every stage after the accepted initial set-backs to the plant's system, such as the yellowing of lower foliage.

Not only will these chemicals create consistency of growth, uniform and early flowering, but also encourage a more dwarf habit and basal branching. The use of a dwarfing agent in the nursery will create a situation whereby an operation may be carried out and completed at one go, for example, pricking out, bedding out, dead heading and so on. Thus, man-hours are reduced and organisation and planning is made simpler, so money is saved. The use of these regulators is not to be encouraged for amateurs, as not only are they very expensive, especially when used on a few plants, but also fairly time consuming, due to the repeated programmes of mixing and applying which must be carried out regularly. As with all horticultural chemicals,

these regulations must be treated with care and respect by both amateur and professional users alike.

The modern hybrid 'geranium' is now firmly established as a bedding plant and the latest varieties are suitable for pot work and hanging containers. Many have a multi-flowering habit and will continue in bloom from mid-summer until late autumn, in fact until the first hard frosts arrive. During the last thirty-five years, many developments have taken place and an extremely competitive market, worth millions of pounds, has grown in producing these F1 'geraniums'. The UK is now a major part of that market, and is presently involved in the skilled research taking place. Hopefully, in five or ten years, many improved types and new varieties will be available.

Fig 32 F1 Hybrid, 'Pulsar Bi-colour'.

## 'OPEN-POLLINATED' VARIETIES OR F2 HYBRIDS

The main advantage of types without a 'blue blooded' ancestry is the low cost of the seed. It is very rare that plants or seedlings are offered from Open-pollinated or F2 Hybrids, because germination is too erratic, growth is uneven and the end product uncertain, regarding flower colour and size. Seed may easily be purchased from seed firms. If an inexpensive and quite colourful display is required and time is of no consequence, try a packet or two, just for fun.

## MINIATURE AND DWARF PELARGONIUMS

Miniature and Dwarf Pelargoniums sprang into popularity in the 1950s in the post-war 'growing for pleasure' era, when people began to have smaller gardens and a few more pounds in their pockets, and when leisure for ordinary gardeners included owning a small greenhouse. These glasshouses were small, so large ornamental plants were edged out of fashion by the 'mini'. During this period, some dedicated *Pelargonium* hybridists had perfected several ideal-sized plants for this purpose. But the first true Miniature Pelargonium was a sport from the old, useful 'Vesuvius' to be known as 'Red Black Vesuvius', followed seven years later by 'Salmon Black Vesuvius'. Both Miniatures are still very popular and perhaps the two varieties most people begin with. Like their parents, but with stronger colouration, these two possess very dark green foliage with a darker zone, and many subsequent varieties of Miniature and Dwarf Pelargoniums follow that trait. Others are in the Ornamental-foliage classification as Bi-colours or Tri-colours, some have a zone as a dark splash in the centre of the foliage, while some do not have a zone at all. Obviously the foliage is smaller than that of the basic Zonal, although in both, the foliage can become fairly large so that sometimes it is difficult to separate the larger Miniatures from the smaller Dwarfs,

and the larger Dwarfs from the basic Zonals. The height of them both has been accepted as a guide together with definite pot sizes, particularly for exhibiting standards. A Miniature's height from the top of the compost to the top of the foliage (it does not matter if the flower head is above this height as long as it is a sensible proportion) should not exceed 5in (13cm). The pot size, at the top of the pot, must not exceed 3½in (9cm). For Dwarfs the sizes are, for the height from compost to top of foliage, more than 5in (12.5cm), but less than 8in (20cm) and pots must be more than 3½in (8.75cm) and must not exceed 4½in (11.5cm).

There are also, quite rarely, those called Micro-miniatures, which should not be attempted by any but the dedicated and experienced pelargonium grower – they are expensive to buy and challenging to grow and propagate. Among these are some tri-coloured leaf forms which are very special, but very difficult. Final

*Fig 33 'Mrs J. C. Mappin' has variegated foliage.*

Fig 34 Miniature Zonal with fancy flowers, 'Baby Bird's Egg'.

pot sizes for Micro-miniatures should be about 2½in (5–6cm), but as long as they are no larger than the Miniatures' pot size for showing with the plant in proportion to the pot size, and with leaves, flowers and height all in proportion also, this will fit in with the accepted classification. Only a few Micro-miniatures are available, and certainly only from a specialist nursery. Miniatures and Dwarfs may be found in small numbers at garden centres, sadly often without a name label, but a specialist would catalogue many varieties from which to choose. They will be a little more expensive than Basic Zonals, but very well worth the extra, especially if you want a special collection.

Cultivation is the same for each of the types of the basic dimensions, however a little more care is needed regarding watering and feeding, because they grow more slowly and, because the habit is dense and stunted, problems with fungal and gall diseases are more common. Propagation is a little tricky, mainly due to the short-jointed (noded) cutting material. Black-leg is also a problem, but clean compost, no over-watering and gentle warmth at the striking stage as well as at potting stages will eliminate this. The plants will give even more pleasure during the winter months if offered adequate light and a temperature of not less than 55°F (13°C) due to their constant wish to flower. The neatness of Miniatures and Dwarfs is an advantage for use on the window-sill indoors at all times, or for a summer display in the window-box, their size and compactness giving no obstruction to the view or to light through the window. There are also Ivy-leaved Miniatures and Dwarfs and Dwarf Regal types available, so a collection of only Miniatures and Dwarfs would permit the grower to enjoy all forms of *Pelargonium* cultivars.

Blooms are either single, semi-double or double, often very large, or more in keeping with the overall size of the plant and foliage, which should be watched when showing because an exhibit must be of a proportionate size, in leaf, flower, height, pot and so on. Almost all the so-called Fancy-flowered types are found in this group – Rosebuds, Bird's Egg, Cactus, Stellars, and even a Miniature Irene have been listed. The colour range is the same as for the basic Zonal, but Miniature and Dwarf Pelargoniums have some of the more unusual colours like magenta and true orange in greater numbers. Many have large markings at the base of their petals, either in a contrasting colour or a white shading which forms a large 'eye' in the complete floret. There are those varieties that have much veining, flecking, striping, spotting, overlaying of other shades and contrasting petal edgings, giving many variations to the blooms.

CHAPTER 5

# Ivy-leaved Pelargoniums

Often known as 'trailing' or 'basket' geraniums, these common names give a clue to their special habit and uses. The early 'Ivies' were developed about three hundred years ago from a wild pelargonium in today's *Dibrachya* section. The principal species from which the Ivy-leaved are derived is *P.peltatum*. The name '*peltatum*', meaning shield-like, refers to the foliage being held on its leaf-stalk (petiole) from a central point on the underside of the leaf and not at the leaf's margin, as in other types, which gives the impression of an umbrella or shield-like formation to the leaf. The common or better-known name is easy to understand because each leaf is shaped just like the ivy or *Hedera helix* with five pointed angular lobes, sometimes having the same aroma as fresh, crushed ivy when its leaves are bruised. In habit,

they also grow, up to a point, like ivy – climbing up, scrambling through or along the ground, over any obstacle. However, pelargoniums do not have suction powers and have to be tied or propped, if an upward growth is required. As natural trailers or scramblers Ivy-leaved Pelargoniums are ideal for hanging baskets, cascading over walls, from tubs, window-boxes or balconies. Their long, wiry, but always brittle stems can each maintain a height or length of many yards. A very effective use for Ivy-leaved Pelargoniums is on the large rockery, or as ground cover during the summer months where they will often root from the nodes that are lying on the soil surface. Slugs and snails can be troublesome here, but a skimming of gravel or crushed egg shells will help to keep them at bay.

The foliage is bright green as a rule and very

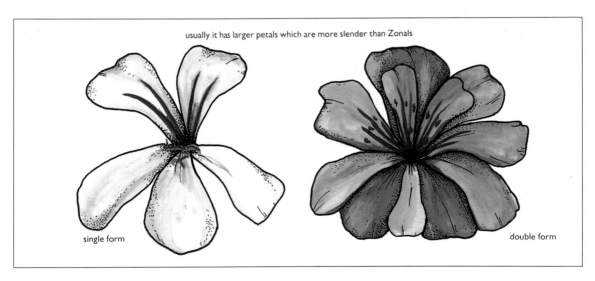

usually it has larger petals which are more slender than Zonals

single form

double form

*Fig 35 Ivy-leaved bloom formation.*

shiny, with or without a zone, or with the zone in the centre of the leaf at the point where, underneath, the petiole joins the leaf-blade. Quite a number of variegated forms also exist and, although these may not bloom so readily, they are attractive. One particular variety, 'L'elegante', is normally discouraged from blooming so that the wonderful medium-sized leaves may show off their variegations which have a pink hue when the plant is grown in bright light and underwatered. This variety has been around for over 120 years and is often grown as a non-flowering house plant.

Hybridisers tend to keep away from Ivy-leaved these days, so most of the varieties available are old, established ones. There have been some additions to the range recently, but the group that took the fancy by storm during the latter part of the 1970s and at the beginning of the 1980s, was developed by means of grafting techniques. The 'mother plant' of the stock is a variety called 'Rouletta' (often wrongly named 'Mexicarin', with various spellings and other incorrect names). This strain is known as the 'Harlequins' and took the white striping in the flowers from the striping of 'Rouletta'. Six varieties of differing reds and pinks were first introduced, including a solitary variety in which the Zonal was used as one of the plants in the grafting, which has a bright orange or red flower with the white stripes becoming suffused with the colour. Work is still going on, and lots of new varieties are becoming available from amateur growers, who are introducing new colours from the mauve spectrum as well as some coloured-leaved forms.

The mature stems of Ivy-leaved do become hard and covered in bark, which will inhibit new shoots and thus flowering stems, so it is best therefore to continually replace stock every second year by taking some cuttings each summer. The flowers are single, semi-double and double, sometimes in a simple form and with florets in each flower head, or umbel, numbering between six and ten, with eight being normal. The natural colour is pale mauve

Fig 36 Ivy-leaved variety 'Harlequin Alpine Glow'.

in the species, so shades of mauve predominate although there are many reds, pinks, magentas, cerises and a few salmons and whites. Striping and flecking is common in modern hybrids, however, ragged petals are more rare.

The 'Harlequins' are newcomers to the type and the popular 'Cascade' types are also fairly new, heralding from the Continent and becoming more popular with Britons holidaying in Europe where they can be seen massed in displays in almost every window and garden.

These 'Cascade' types have small to medium

blooms which are single and of a primitive shape, but are so floriferous, especially the varieties with whitish stems, that their smallness is counterbalanced by the quantity of blooms. The flowers are quite self-shattering, which is an advantage in damp climates because the problems set off by dead and dying blooms left on plants can spoil a whole display. Foliage is shiny and also small, which is also a plus with hanging or trailing types growing in a windy situation – often the case with hanging baskets and high window-boxes.

Most of the 'Ivies' hold their blooms on long, sometimes brittle, stalks, high above or away from the foliage. The brittle stems will root very easily even if just snapped off at a node and set in some suitable rooting medium. It is unfortunate that this brittle tendency, useful in some respects, mars the chance of transporting to shows and exhibitions safely, so 'Ivies' are not as popular on the show scene as other members of the family. The use of canes on the show bench is allowed as long as it is unobtrusive, but stronger canes or equipment will be needed for safety during transit and will have to be removed carefully at staging time. However, after taking all these precautions, and being awarded a prize in this class, you will feel that all your effort was well worthwhile.

Zonal Pelargoniums have been used in hybridising with 'Ivies' to create what is termed as the 'Hybrid Ivy'. There are a dozen or so varieties available, including one of the 'Harlequin' range, and some with heavily veined petals. There is also a golden, variegated form of these more upright, but still semi-pendulous varieties, which were first introduced by a French hybridiser and nurseryman, Victor Lemoine, in about 1890. It is a very strong-growing plant which is short noded and with large leaves that are usually softer, light green with little or no zone. The blooms are larger and of the normal 'Ivy' colours available with the present exception of magenta.

Most Ivy-leaved varieties, apart from a few

*Fig 37 Fancy-flowered Ivy-leaved variety 'Pink Carnation'.*

'specials', can be purchased easily from all nurseries and garden centres in late spring. As a rule the common ones are good value for money, giving lasting colour in return for little attention in many outside situations, until the first damaging frost. Their usefulness indoors is limited due to the size and lengthy habit, but Miniature and Dwarf forms now available should fill this gap. In many large and heated conservatories, 'Ivy-leaved' varieties can be seen growing up into the roof-light and will most likely have been growing in the greenhouse beds for many years, always flowering at all times of the year. Take care that dropped leaves and blooms or petals are removed regularly from such plants to keep pests and diseases at bay. Greenfly is the main pest of the 'Ivy-leaf', colonising at the new tips of each branch.

# CHAPTER 6

# Beginning

You can buy, beg and be given plants, or produce them at home from your own existing stock, or from other people's stocks. Purchasing pelargoniums is the easiest way to start up or swell a collection, but it is not as exciting as propagating and creating a new plant at home.

Where can you buy pelargoniums? It may be that you have the good fortune to live close to a specialist nursery; this is by far the best place to choose and buy the plants. Here, thousands of plants of different types and varieties will be on show and for sale. Because the owner and the staff are themselves specialists in growing pelargoniums, you should be assured of good quality specimens. No dedicated nurseryman will object to a few questions being asked by a prospective customer such as 'What type of compost is used?', 'How often, if ever, have the young plants been fed and with what type of fertiliser?' and 'How long has the plant been potted up?'. The answers will help when the plants are brought home so that compost may be of a similar nature, the feeding regime and the potting on timing may be similar to that which the young plant has been used to.

In choosing a plant at the nursery, it is wise to

*Fig 38 'Jasmin' (Jasmine) a very young plant of this Regal variety.*

walk around first, taking in all the varieties on offer before actually choosing. Make sure each plant has a label. Take note of the size and obvious vitality of the plant and of the state of the compost – is there moss growing on the surface? Does the soil look powdery and new? These factors will tell you how long the plant has been in the pot. Powdery soil will mean that the cutting or plant is newly potted so you should leave it well alone until the plant has developed a stronger root system in the new compost. Many people will buy a plant in flower, which will often not be the best of the bunch, but because it has a flower, it cannot be resisted. It would be much wiser to purchase a strong, stocky plant with buds but without open flowers, since buds show that a plant is capable of blooming. Foliage should be of a size which is relevant to the variety or type, and should be of a good colour, again relevant to the variety.

Look for signs of pests, diseases and disorders as it is often difficult for a large nursery to track down every insect among so many plants. Stems should be strong and straight until the pinching-out point and then new branching should be even in growth and position. Take care that there is no damage to the stem at all. This, more than anything, will be detrimental to a good specimen.

You must bear in mind for what purpose you require the plant – is it for exhibition, for bedding, for greenhouse or conservatory display? The siting of your greenhouse or conservatory is important when choosing some plants. For example, there is no point in buying varieties like Ornamental-foliage types if the glasshouse never has shading and is always in full sun during the height of a summer afternoon, nor is it of any use to choose plants that grow large and vigorous for a small greenhouse, nor to buy plants with naturally large, soft foliage suitable for bedding purposes in the UK. For exhibition or show plants, select those which are naturally self-branching and floriferous, taking care to make sure that the chosen plant fits easily into recognised show schedules. A hanging

basket in a very exposed situation will require a variety with smallish foliage and short internodal length. It may be that you are planning a trained plant, such as a plant grown on a standard stem. In this case, choose a plant with a strong upright tendency that has not been stopped or pinched out so that the stem may grow on unchecked until the desired height is reached. So, choosing the type and variety carefully is very important.

When arriving home put your acquisitions in a shaded part of the greenhouse or similar environment for a few days. Don't be tempted to work on them until they have become accustomed to their new situation. Perhaps it would be wise to remove all the open flowers if any are present – a very painful task for the grower! Carefully remove any damaged and naturally yellowing leaves. Give tepid water if necessary by plunging the pot into a tray of water rather than watering from the surface, let the plant have a good soak, then remove it and allow it to drain. After the first few days, the plant may be integrated into your collection, after a careful examination for any pests and so on that may have developed during this period.

Many people have no alternative but to buy their plants by mail order from a nursery a distance from home. Many specialist nurseries advertise in the gardening press and in the journals of specialist societies. The usual procedure is to apply for a catalogue costing very little and then choose from the lists available, sending the money with the order back to the nursery. As you cannot see what is for sale, it is even more important to choose the right plants for your situations by observing other collections and attending shows. Also reading articles and books will help you to become acquainted with each variety desired. The next step is to complete the order form, after reading the nursery's terms and conditions of sale. The cost of a common variety, as a rooted cutting, will be very cheap, but if it is more special, it will be a little dearer. Varieties introduced in the current year will be perhaps six or seven times

*Fig 39 It is easy to see why Regals are often known as 'Show Pelargoniums'.*

the basic price, reducing in price each year after. An acknowledgement of order, a delivery date and answers to questions about compost, feeding and so on will usually be supplied by the nursery on receipt of a stamped addressed envelope. Plants may be wrapped in newspaper or corrugated paper with some method of retaining the compost by means of pads of paper or other material, and the completed order packed into cardboard cartons, or specially formed polystyrene boxes, with cells able to house small pots or peat pellets and the two halves taped ready for transportation.

Parcels are transported by rail, road or by the postal service with most plants arriving at their destination within a few days. The majority of nurseries time despatch in order to avoid a weekend in transit.

Now comes the exciting part! The package has arrived. Some carriers ask for a signature and it is a good idea also to mark the receipt form with the word 'unexamined', as well as the recipient's signature, particularly if someone else takes receipt of the parcel. This could save a great deal of trouble if the parcel has been delayed, or the contents damaged. If you are worried that the carrier might call when no one is at home ask a neighbour to take receipt of the parcel and ask the nursery to note the alternative delivery address on the address label. Don't allow plants to be left on the doorsteps while you are on holiday. Some carriers will take parcels back to the depot if there is no answer at the address, so an alternative address or an instruction to leave the parcel in an outhouse will prevent the parcel sitting in the depot all weekend.

Although the parcel may be marked 'This Way Up', this is very seldom possible during the journey, so open the box with care and, after removing the plants from the wrappings, making certain that all name labels are with each plant, check for those in distress from the darkness or perhaps the cold, as well as the lack of air circulation. Remove any dead or damaged foliage and all flowers, then place the plants in a shaded and suitably warm place (not hot) for a few days. They may require water by plunging into a tray of tepid water, but not unless the compost is powder dry. Check for pests and diseases too. After a day or so, the plants will become their lively selves again. Now, if you wish, they can be potted into a suitable compost and larger pots. If the plants or cuttings are growing in peat pots or peat pellets, these will need to be carefully removed where possible, but if the roots are likely to be damaged, leave that area of peat pot intact. Peat pots or pellets often become very dry and will not absorb moisture using normal methods so leave them to soak for an hour before removing, draining and potting up. It is vital that these peat products are moistened before any potting up or potting on is completed.

*Fig 40* P.violareum, *synonym* P.tri-colour arborea. *The foliage is a pointed oval shape and is grey in colour. The foliage shown here is of* P.filicifolium *type.*

Many kinds of pelargoniums may be purchased locally from a nearby greengrocer or nursery. In this situation, the plants are purchased generally from a grower or plant wholesaler and sold at the shop. Many of these outlets *do* have knowledgeable staff who can help with advice, but is unusual to find plants labelled. Also, the practice of enveloping the plant in non-porous sleeves is not good for pelargoniums, if they are to remain inside the sleeve for any length of time. All sorts of problems can occur in this enclosed environment, such as leaves and flowers dying and the plant becoming open to fungal attacks. It is often difficult to inspect the plant thoroughly, but if the shop assistant is willing to remove the sleeve or wrapping to enable an inspection and this proves satisfactory, then by all means purchase your find. It is usually mature plants that are offered for sale, and they will have been in the pot for a fair period. This suggests that a feeding programme should be implemented once the plant has acclimatised to the new surroundings. The prices charged will vary, depending on whether the plants are grown locally, but a young mature plant could be well worth the money.

The most obvious place to purchase a pelargonium locally is at a garden centre. Usually, pelargoniums are not grown on the premises, but delivered by van from a grower at regular intervals. Some garden centres are well known for selling good quality pelargoniums, but many places do not insist that the plant be labelled by the grower which does deter those who actually collect plants from buying. They may often be arranged on benching in a greenhouse that is not always tailor-made for pelargoniums and are placed close together because space is at a premium. Care must be taken when inspecting for problems as the plants are usually close-noded and large-leaved which impairs the passage of air through the plants. Large plants are normally sold in bloom, and some garden centres buy in small-rooted cuttings early in the year, and grow them on into large pots to be ready for late spring selling. F1 seedlings will be found almost exclusively at garden centres as small plants just out of the seedling stage and, more often, growing in peat pellets or punnets containing up to six plantlets. These are a good buy and an ideal way to create a bedding scheme outdoors when the season is ready.

More and more venues are selling pot plants these days, from roadside cabins to garage forecourts, and here much more care should be taken before even considering a buy. These plants were grown in a nursery and delivered perhaps days ago to the seller, they may be placed outside in all weathers, draughts and fuel fumes. It is possible to do a little detective work if you really want a variety from this type of source. Find out when the next consignment is due, and purchase within a day or two of their arrival, or even meet the delivery van, in order to be more certain of getting a good plant. Again it is likely to be swathed in plastic, so ask for this to be removed before purchasing. Plants on display at this type of venue are offered to 'impulse buyers' who stop for snacks, petrol or a rest from travelling and prices may be too high for the quality of the plant, but you may find exceptions.

Jumble and car boot sales are also chancy places from which to buy plants, because, unless the grower is known, it is impossible to be sure that the plant was grown in hygienic conditions. Make certain the specimen is clear of any visual ailments – it would probably be safer to keep the plant away from others for a while. It is likely that the stall-holder will know the variety, even though it will perhaps not be labelled, so do ask as it is much more interesting to know the name of a plant. Many a fantastic variety has been bought from a jumble sale!

Any plant given as a gift or as a swop should also go through the 'third degree'. Never ask for cuttings from suspect stock, however desirable they may appear and never give away swops or cuttings from a suspect plant yourself as horticultural disasters are embarrassing.

# CHAPTER 7

# Pots, Composts and Potting

## POTS

Once your plant is safely home and acclimatised to its new surroundings, the temptation to 'do something' with it will prove very strong. Pots should be scrupulously clean if they have previously been used, and be sound and in good condition. In fact it is a good idea to inspect and thoroughly clean all pots when emptying them, before storing them in a clean place – this way a good wash will be all that is required. If a plant dies from an unknown cause, it may be better to discard its pot rather than using it for another plant.

Clay pots should be given particular care and attention as they are extremely porous and a crack can go unnoticed, thus allowing bacteria to thrive. It is vital too, that all clay containers, whether decorative urns or ordinary flower pots, should be soaked for an hour or two before use, so that the dried clay will not take water from the compost. Crocking is also necessary with clay pots, by covering the holes with small, very clean pieces of broken clay pot or pebbles. The bases of the clay pots sit firmly on the ground or benching, therefore not allowing any surplus water to escape easily, so placing pieces over the holes in the base of the pot will prevent soil from escaping, and also provide a drainage area. Some old clay pots and urns have holes which extend a way up the outside wall of the pot. These are ideal and enable excess water to run away. By placing a shallow scattering of gravel underneath the clay pot and standing it on a flat, solid surface, drainage will be improved. Do not imagine that crocking will stop insects from entering the pot through the hole. The best way to stop pests from entering through drainage holes is to cut pieces from close gauge plastic netting (the type used for greenhouse shading and crop production), but even then smaller insects will sometimes be able to find a way in. Clay pots suit pelargoniums better than plastic pots, as the porosity of clay encourages the passage of air through the compost and also helps to prevent the problem of overwatering, which all pelargoniums hate. Clay also looks much more natural than plastic, particularly for use out in the garden or the patio. Unfortunately, they are heavy, especially when filled with compost, they can damage easily if dropped or knocked, are more expensive, not always perfectly hygienic and do take up more space when stacked.

Most *Pelargonium* growers use plastic pots these days and growing methods have been adjusted accordingly. Fortunately, most pelargoniums are reasonably accommodating when it comes to change, and don't mind growing in plastic containers. Plastic pots are easier to clean and dry and they can be purchased in many colours, but terracotta looks more natural and balances with plant colour nicely. The compost used in plastic pots should always be of a more open consistency to eliminate possible waterlogging caused by overwatering, and to allow the air, incorporated in the compost, to remain. Drainage holes are more numerous,

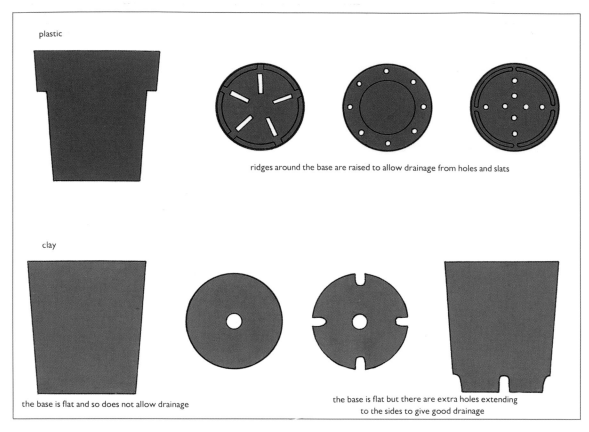

plastic

ridges around the base are raised to allow drainage from holes and slats

clay

the base is flat and so does not allow drainage

the base is flat but there are extra holes extending to the sides to give good drainage

*Fig 41 Types of pots and drainage facilities.*

and at the base there are raised ribs or feet which lift the pot off any surface, allowing adequate drainage. Crocking is not necessary and takes up valuable compost and root space. It should only be done if you need to stabilise the plant and pot.

Plastic pots are much thinner in construction, and store more easily; they are also very much lighter in weight and are more durable and better for cleaning purposes. A solution of Jeyes Fluid (5 dessertspoons to each gallon of water) in which clay pots and crocks should be soaked and then scrubbed and plastic pots and labels washed will ensure a clean pot ready to receive the plant. Any wooden containers intended for plants should also be treated in this solution. It is vital that all porous materials should be allowed to drain and left to dry thoroughly and re-soaked before use. Never use Jeyes Fluid on polystyrene products, but

wash these expanded polystyrene trays, boxes and modules often used as seed boxes or for cuttings with a soap solution similar to household washing-up liquid, if cleaning is required. Polystyrene containers are mainly used once by commercial growers, so the hygiene problem will not arise, but as all gardeners hate to throw things away, they are sometimes used again and can, in fact, be purchased from gardening stores. The advantage of polystyrene being a good conductor of temperature is an asset in warm temperatures, but be careful when these products have been in icy conditions, if you are planning to use them for plants and seeds. When propagating, the roots will find their way to the warmer shell of the trays, and if seedlings, cuttings or plants are not potted up before the roots find their way into the pockets of the expanded polystyrene, their roots will be damaged when you remove them.

Other pots which are used only for one crop are the tarred paper types known as 'whale-hide', which are used by commercial growers, perhaps more often these days only for the production of young tomato plants. If plants are purchased or grown in paper pots, it is best to carefully remove the pot before planting or potting up the plant, so that root run can begin immediately.

It is sometimes tempting to use containers not specifically produced for plant cultivation, such as discarded disposable drinking cups, yoghurt and cream cartons, and so on. These are far from ideal for a number of reasons. Normally pale brown or white in colour and very thin, you will see when holding them up to the light, that the light will be able to reach the roots which is not natural at all, either for a pelargonium or any other plant. They may also

be top-heavy which could cause the plant to topple, there will be no raised feet and no holes at the base. All growing pots need holes, so you will have to burn, pierce or drill holes yourself. Is it worthwhile when you can buy pleasant-coloured, economically-priced plastic pots anywhere? Clay, plastic and the more modern forms of synthetic fabrics have been evaluated above; but wire and wooden-slatted holders as well as metal containers are also used extensively and some of these and others will be discussed in Chapter 10.

Most pots come in many sizes, from a tiny thimble to massive urns. Generally, the larger the pot the easier it will be to manage the plant, but the unwritten rule 'never over-pot a pelargonium' must be remembered. Having ensured that a clean, dry, correct-sized pot is available, a label and a waterproof marker will be the next

*Fig 42 A hanging basket, newly planted with variegated* nepeta *and Ivy-leaved Pelargoniums 'Rouletta' and 'Yale'.*

requisite. Plastic labels also come in many sizes and colours. Some colours are rather bright and strong, so unless various colours are needed for identification purposes, choose white or soft green as they are less distracting. Metal labels, which are mainly of aluminium, are popular and more durable than plastic which can shatter with age and light exposure. Lead-type pencils or purchased letter dyes are used for marking. Choose a size suitable for the plant and pot, making sure the label is long or large enough to cope with the variety name and other data thought important enough to record such as cutting, potting date, type of compost, and so on. Ordinary lead-type pencils are fairly reliable, but a good waterproof and sunproof marker pen with a very fine point is best. Try hard to discover the correct name of the variety and label all plants in a collection. The correct labelling of specimens can only encourage others to grow particular varieties, as well as making life easy when it comes to knowing your own collection.

## COMPOSTS

Up to this point, the word 'compost' has been used many times in this book. No doubt some beginners may be a little confused, as to many 'compost' is a recycled mass of organic household rubbish to be dug into the garden soil to add humus. This is, up to a point, quite correct. So what do greenhouse plant growers mean when they talk about compost? They really mean a sowing, potting or planting medium which is known nowadays as 'potting compost'. They are not really 'potting or sowing soils' either, because they are all something more than that, although the majority of those suitable for the *Pelargonium* do contain some soil. A beginner-grower is more likely to purchase a soil-based potting compost instead of mixing their own concoction at home. All soils and composts must be sterilised, which is time- as well as space-consuming and may require the

purchase of special equipment and a form of dry or steam heat. Experts do still occasionally mix and make up their own special recipes, particularly those who prefer peat-based or soilless mediums.

First, what is a potting medium and what is its use? A plant needs something in which to anchor itself and to retain moisture until it is needed, a material that will keep the medium open and allow air to be present as well as allow free drainage, and something to hold and contain all the basic nutrients and important trace elements. In the open ground or garden, animal life in the soil assists in keeping the soil near perfect for planting, with a few additives put into the soil from time to time by the gardener. For plants in pots this is not the case, so extra care must be taken to enrich the soil or compost, as well as adjusting it to the specific needs of individual specimens. Plants in pots are fairly helpless creatures, with the grower as dictator and provider!

It is unwise to use garden soil for a potting mix or potting compost, even if it has been sterilised to kill all pests, weed seeds and bacteria – in fact, not all kinds of bacteria should be eradicated, as there are those which are beneficial. Most purchased potting mixes have been carefully heat treated so as not to kill the advantageous life in the soil. The soil content of compost is loam. Good loam is produced by stacking upturned pasture-land turf with farm-yard manure into large, neat piles, watering it well, covering it with a waterproof cover and leaving it for half a year or longer. When the loam is ready for sterilising and mixing with other ingredients it should be crumbly yet retain its shape when squeezed. John Innes formula composts, coded Nos 1, 2 and 3, and a seed sowing mixture, are the main soil-based composts which are readily available. This recognised formula is fairly standardised, the only difference being the quality and state of the loam in each manufacturer's mix. Loam gives the mixture body and supplies clay, humus and decomposed organic matter and has a pH

*Fig 43 'Duke of Edinburgh'.*

reading which is slightly acid (pH is a scale used to signify the acidity or alkalinity of any material).

Coarse washed sand, moss peat, chalk, limestone and superphosphates (powdered hoof and horn) and also potash (the two latter ingredients in varying amounts depending on the mix required) are mixed with the loam. No 1 is a weaker formula than the No 3 formula. For semi-mature and mature pelargoniums, John Innes No 2 is suitable. There are loam-free potting mixes, or peat-based composts available. For pelargoniums, peat-based composts are not ideal, and the natural habitat of the *Pelargonium* bears out this statement. Many pelargonium nurseries use peat-based composts today, as commercial-cuttings root more quickly in peat-based mediums and grow faster initially in this type of compost, so becoming saleable items in a shorter time. However, if a plant is to grow naturally and live out its recognised life-span, it will need the potting medium to be as natural as possible.

Automatic potting and pot-filling machines used in larger nurseries do not work with a loam heavy compost, and many nurseries send plants through the post, so a lighter compost such as a peat compost is required to keep down the cost of transport. This also makes carrying trays of plants around the nursery less of a toil. However, this lack of weight may be a problem when plants become tall, and if a quantity of gravel is added to the compost it might stop the plant from falling over, but it will take up volume that could be filled with nutritious compost. As well as not being a natural medium for pelargoniums, peat-based compost will become very difficult to water if allowed to become very dry. Some peat-based products now include a moisture-retaining element which keeps the soil wet on watering, as well as ensuring that moisture remains in the compost rather than running quickly down the pot and through the drainage holes if the mixture has become too dry. Always remember that pelargoniums do not like to be very wet. Other

55

Fig 44 'Prince of Orange'; this tidy and compact scented-leaf variety has a strong orange-citrus aroma.

problems that have become more common with the widespread introduction of peat-based mediums are that the sciarid fly enjoys living in peat composts and also that the vine weevil lays its eggs in peat compost; these hatch into the larvae which then cause considerable damage to young roots.

Proprietary soilless or peat-based composts contain the necessary nutrients and trace elements and these are also available to the amateur for making both types of composts at home. Although peat-based composts are easier to make from sphagnum moss peat, which should have been heat-treated by the producer at the baling stage, the amateur grower and beginner will find that a soil-based compost will prove easier to understand and work with, and produce a healthy pelargonium.

## POTTING

Now that pots are at hand and a good quality compost available, the task of potting can begin. Potting can be divided into four different operations: (1) **potting up** is the action of placing a new seedling or rooted cutting into a new pot and new compost, which is often of a stronger formula than previously; (2) **potting on** is the gradual increasing of the pot size and perhaps strength of the compost, as each plant becomes more mature; and (3) **re-potting** is the term used when a mature or semi-mature plant is in its final pot which requires the compost to be replenished while keeping the plant in the same pot. Re-potting is best carried out in early spring, just before new, fresh growth is evident. Usually, this is done in alternate years and is combined

56

with the careful removal and replacement of the top compost during the intervening year.

Sometimes a plant and pot cannot be moved because it is too large, or it is in a place where it is growing up or through some permanent trellis-work, or it is attached to a wall. The plant can be given fertiliser to replenish the nutrients, but there is nothing like good fresh potting compost to give a plant a new lease of life. The ideal solution is to take out, very carefully and not going too near the stem of the plant, a slice of the compost, fill the triangular area with new compost and do not water for a day or two until the cut roots have sealed. This operation may be carried out each spring, moving the area to be replaced around the base of the plant. It is advisable to take out about one-eighth of the soil each time, but feed and water as normal during the remainder of the year. If the plant is situated in a restricted or long-established greenhouse bed, the same procedure may be adopted if it is impractical to

remove and replace the complete bed every few years.

Finally, there is (4) **_de-potting_** which is moving a plant into a smaller sized pot.

## Potting Up

When removing seedlings and newly-rooted cuttings, it is vital that root damage is minimal. Always hold the seedlings or plantlet by the leaves and as far as possible avoid holding the stem, because any damage to the stem tissue, even perspiration or bruising from the fingers, will allow bacterial diseases to enter the wound – the plant may be able to produce a replacement leaf, but cannot replace a stem.

Before any potting operation, collect together all the equipment you require: compost; labels; label marker; pots; soil additives; a tray without holes to act as a reservoir; tepid water with a fungicide added for new seedlings and cuttings; and a small kitchen fork, larger

*Fig 45 'Deacon Bonanza'.*

fork or similar for removing cuttings. Arrange all these on a clean, spacious work surface. First, deal with the compost. If it has been purchased it will definitely require tipping out on to the work surface and mixing; any lumps must be rubbed in the hands or sieved. If the compost is peat-based or loam-based to the John Innes formula No 1 it is suitable for young seedlings and cuttings, but it will be necessary to incorporate some extra drainage material for pelargoniums. For tiny plants and seedlings drainage material should be coarse, washed horticultural sand, never builders' sand or 'acquired' sand and grit from roadside winter silos as this will probably have had salt added. Other additives such as Perlite or Fullasorb may be used to absorb moisture and keep the compost 'open' and allow better drainage. Mix in about one-eighth of coarse sand or the other suggested elements, or a mixture of both, to one volume of compost and sieve the mixture in your hands for a few minutes to incorporate air.

The next step is to take a clean pot, fill it partially and tamp down lightly either with an especially made rammer, or with the base of another clean pot. Arrange the plantlet on the top of the compost making sure that the soil level will be the same as it was in its previous situation. Gently apply the compost round the plant until the pot is full to the rim, then tap down on the bench. Never ram down on the soil after the plant is in place or use your thumbs to press down the compost around the stem, because any hard particles or fingernails could damage the stem, resulting in fungal problems later, or shearing off roots with the downward pressing action.

Write the name of the variety with a waterproof pen or pencil on the label and insert into the pot. At this stage, the growing tip is removed by using a razor-sharp knife and nicking out the tip very carefully. This is called 'pinching out', and can be done with the fingernails, but the knife method is much safer. If the plant is destined for a trained shape, only pinch out if required for the beginning of the shaping.

Stand the pot in a reservoir of tepid water until water is seen on the compost surface, remove the pot and allow it to drain. You will see that the compost has sunk gradually with the soaking, and the compost should be tucked around the roots, expelling all air pockets and leaving a space between the top of the compost and the pot rim of about ½in (1cm). Subsequent watering operations can therefore be thorough and no water or compost will wash over the pot edge. After they have drained, stand the plants in a warm, sheltered and slightly shaded place for a day or two, gradually moving them into the more well-lit areas of the greenhouse, conservatory or window-sill to grow on. More pinching out may be required before the next stage.

## Potting On

When the plant has developed well and outgrown its first pot, it will be 'bursting at the seams' and will require to be potted on into a larger one. Do *not* over-pot pelargoniums, as they will be reluctant to flower if not confined. Pinching out is again advised. Choose a scrupulously clean pot one or two sizes larger than before. If you are going to use a clay pot this time, do not forget to soak the pot and put in the crocks beforehand. The compost may now be a stronger type of John Innes, perhaps No 2 or the equivalent, again add some form of extra drainage material which can now be larger, such as horticultural grit. The addition of Perlite or Fullasorb will also be beneficial. Rub and sieve the compost through the fingers as before. Place crocks over the base holes if you need to. Fill the pot to the level needed to receive the plant and press it down gently. Hold the small plastic pot between both palms and roll gently to loosen the compost, turn the pot upside-down and the contents will fall into the hands without the root-ball disintegrating. A sharp tap on the bench with the edge of the upturned pot may be necessary, but it is best avoided in case the young roots are damaged as well as creating a mess from the loose compost. Place the still intact root-ball and compost into the pot and fill in round the outside with new compost to the rim, tap down and place in the reservoir of clean, tepid water. Don't forget to replace the label and check that the writing is still legible. After draining, leave the plant in a shaded place for a few days to allow it to recover. A more mature plant will take longer to overcome any disturbance, so do not rush into putting your newly-potted plant on to the staging in full sunlight.

## Re-potting and De-potting

Re-potting should take place when the old compost is exhausted, or has become sour, when the plant has become root- or pot-bound, or when root problems are suspected. When re-potting a healthy plant, it will not be necessary to break up the root-ball, but gently teasing out a little of the compost with a pointed stick, or a plastic or lacquered chopstick, will enable the roots to find their way into the new compost easily. The task can be done at any time, just before or when the plant is in active growth. Of course it would be foolhardy to re-pot a plant during the approach to a show or display or when a propagation session is to take place in the near future. When the root-ball has to be broken up it is better to re-pot just before active growth starts, so that any damage to roots and any old roots that are pruned can be replaced by new ones at the onset of the growing period. When an older plant has lost its vigour and is beginning to look tired, this will usually be a sign that the plant needs new compost because feeding will not have the same success as re-potting.

Re-potting is carried out the same way as potting-on but into the final-sized pot required, simultaneously doing any pruning or pinching out as necessary. The final pot size must be considered carefully, especially if showing in competitions is envisaged, taking care that the size does not exceed the generally recognised

Fig 46 'Magalluf' has pretty foliage too.

maximum pot size. Do not over-pot or use such a large pot that you will have difficulty in transporting it. Sometimes a plant will be taken from a large pot, the soil teased away, new soil introduced and the plant re-potted into the same pot after it has been cleaned, or into a new pot of the same size.

It may also be necessary occasionally to **de-pot**, that is to plant in a pot smaller than the original. When de-potting, root pruning is needed and then the plant is shaken lightly or the roots teased to remove most of the spent compost before fresh compost is introduced. This can be a drastic step for the plant so take care with the recovery procedure. Plants brought from the garden at the onset of frost in the autumn are frequently de-potted to house the well-developed root system built up during a summer outside into pots that can be managed during the winter months in a frost-free house. This can be quite traumatic for *Pelargonium* and it might be a good idea to take some cuttings from the variety just to be sure of new plants if the mother plant does not recover.

# CHAPTER 8

# General Cultivation

## BASICS

Regular attention and good husbandry are of paramount importance to ensure success in growing ideal specimens of any type or variety of *Pelargonium*. Every plant *should* be examined each day. This, of course, is not actually possible; nevertheless, plants should be looked over as often as you can, to prevent the spread of any problems. Daily viewings will give the grower a better knowledge of how each plant differs in growth, habit and requisites from its neighbour, even though conditions are the same – thus gaining the type of experience often referred to as 'green fingers'. A specimen may be in dire need of re-potting, cuttings may have rooted or seeds germinated, or watering may be required, and a decision is needed, on the very day that the collection is not observed.

Pelargoniums will need to be housed in a heated greenhouse or conservatory or perhaps a well-lit window area, during the cooler months even in some milder climates because nights can be cold, and pelargoniums generally will not tolerate any frost. Very occasionally, during extremely mild winters or in very sheltered regions, it is possible to over-winter them in the garden, but it is wiser to presume that they will need winter protection with some warmth. Over-wintering is always a problem and is perhaps the main reason that deters the wider use of pelargoniums by the average gardener. Assuming that a heated greenhouse is not available, what is to be done with your plants during the colder months? First, deal with those plants used for bedding in the garden, either in the open ground or in pots, and so

on. As an insurance, a week or two before they should be lifted, in September, take a few cuttings from each variety, preferably from a shoot with no blooms. These cuttings can be treated (*see* Chapter 9) and then placed on a well-lit window-sill. Interest during the darker months will intensify when it becomes apparent that the cuttings have developed a root system. Pot first into small pots, then into larger pots until it is safe to put them permanently outside.

*Fig 47 The National Pelargonium Collection at Fibrex Nurseries in Worcestershire.*

Fig 48 A park bedding scheme using double Zonals. Almost all types of the family will lend themselves to garden planting in frost-free periods.

All plants, whether from the greenhouse or from the home, will require a period of 'hardening off', as it is descriptively termed, before the final planting is made. This means a gentle and steady introduction to the outside environment and temperature. If a coldframe is used, plants may be placed in the frame on sunny spring days, but at the beginning they should have the lights shut or some similar protection, until after a day or two, the lights may be left off. Each evening the plants should be taken into the warmth until nights are not threatening a low temperature. If no coldframe or cold greenhouse is available, take the plants outside (standing them on a hard surface so that worms and insects cannot gain entry through the pot-base holes) and follow on the acclimatising programme just as with a coldframe. The plants will take on an amazingly healthy, lively look after a few days of natural surroundings and fresh air.

If you have the spare space, pot up the plants from the garden before the frosts, which are usually in the first week of October in the mid-southern UK (however, frosts have been known to occur earlier and later, so it is prudent to listen to weather forecasts). Lift the plants very carefully with a fork, shaking off most of the garden soil without damaging roots, then re-pot with John Innes No 2 compost. If the plants are of a lush and large growth (and they probably will be), it may be wise to cut away some of the larger leaves and cut back the plant. As with pruning, any seepage of moisture from the wound should be dabbed with Captan dust or similar. Put the plants in a warm, shaded place for a few days, then take them indoors or into the greenhouse or conservatory, to be enjoyed throughout the winter. As long as the temperature of the area does not fall below freezing point your plants will be comfortable. On the market, there are various artificial lighting units that will keep plants happy throughout the over-wintering period, provided that the instructions regarding the height of the light unit and other special factors are adhered to. These units come in a number of forms, from attractive pieces of furniture to a specially-manufactured light bulb for horticultural use. Prices are fairly high, but you may decide that the outlay is justified.

## WATERING

If it is possible to keep the growing area above 7°C–10°C (45°F–50°F) and provided there is adequate light, many flowers will be produced throughout the winter months. The extra flowering encouraged will mean that the plant needs more water and a little weak liquid feed, but do not overwater it. As a general rule plants kept in cold conditions and allowed just to 'tick over' until the spring will need watering perhaps only once a month until spring approaches, the days become warmer and light becomes greater. If in doubt, don't water a *Pelargonium*, as there are many more which perish through over-watering than through underwatering. Always water the plant with tepid water and either stand the can in the warm greenhouse, or add some hot water from the tap to the can before using. In the past, it was always stated that rain-water was best and more natural, but with today's polluted atmosphere, this may now be open to question. If, however, you are certain that your collected rain-water is clean and pure, then it will be more beneficial to the plants, but if it is years since that old water butt was cleaned out, a solution of Jeyes Fluid of 1 tsp (5ml) to 1 gallon (5 litres) for soil watering (for spraying, halve the quantity of Jeyes Fluid) will help to eradicate any harmful microscopic creatures that may live in it. Tap water varies from area to area in both chemical and lime content and it is these factors that usually worry growers into using rain- or pond-water, but if the water is drawn about eight hours before use and left to stand, much of these additives will evaporate. Remember that if water is drawn from the hot tap, some of the lime content will also have adhered to the hot water system.

The way a plant is watered can be important. A new seedling will easily become dislodged if the jet of water is too harsh. It has been said that pelargoniums do not relish being sprayed too often, so a gentle trickle with a small-bore spout around the outside wall of the pot will ensure that the outer compost is kept moist. This will encourage the roots to spread to the outside of the compost so that they can reach this moisture. The same technique is also applicable for larger and mature plants. Try to avoid any overhead spraying that could be necessary in the cold, still, dark months, or when the sun is at its height in the midday period or on hot, bright days, and never spray or water last thing at night! On the odd occasions when a

*Fig 49 Angel variety, 'Swedish Angel'.*

plant has been allowed to become very dry or was perhaps purchased in a dry state, it will be useless to try to water it with conventional methods. The only way to ensure that the roots are properly watered, will be to plunge the pot into a water-bath for an hour or so, or until the top of the soil begins to show a water level. Then drain it well before shading and placing it back in the collection. This is by far the best method of watering as a normal task if you have only a few plants.

Automatic watering systems are now quite common in the amateur's greenhouse. Generally they are not suitable for pelargoniums mainly because they like to be fairly dry before being watered, which is not possible with automatic systems. Each plant will often require water at different times and in differing amounts depending on its type, variety or size of plant and growing regime, and again this is not possible with these systems. Individual watering is much more realistic and also gives the grower an opportunity to inspect his or her plants. Automatic watering can, of course, be useful when holidays are taken and a willing 'caretaker' cannot be found.

Holidays or even weekend breaks can present a real problem. Plants will not become stressed without feed for two weeks, but in the hot weather they will become stressed without water. To guard against total dehydration it is a good idea to move greenhouse plants outside to a shady place, perhaps under some trees or shrubs which will create cooler surroundings. Plants in large pots, patio tubs, window-boxes and the like can be treated in this way. It may be wise to provide a saucer or tray of water to help the plant through this period of neglect, depending on how long that period will be. Hanging baskets, certainly, will need a tray of water in which to stand because even if it does rain the water will drain away through the basket. Do not forget to sprinkle a few slug pellets or granules around to protect plants standing on soil or in a place likely to be attractive to slugs and snails. These preventive measures will keep a plant safely moist for two to three weeks in most summers in the UK. In the winter, of course, watering should not be too much of a problem, apart from extended absences. A large reservoir of cotton 'wicks' can be rigged up with wick trailing from the water to each pot and being embedded 1in (2.5cm) or so into the compost ensuring a water supply until the reservoir becomes empty. So, if a willing neighbour can care for the greenhouse only at the weekend, this could provide your answer. Plants bedded outside in the border will not need any extra care apart from the scattering of a slug killer or preventer, if you think it is necessary.

Your plants will also benefit from a holiday, so take off all flowers and opening buds (in addition to the normal picking over of dead and dying flowers and leaves) and any buds that will open before the grower's return home. Do not forget to give some shade in the greenhouse if your holiday will be during the height of the hot, sunny season, and try to leave at least one window ajar. Automatic louvre windows may be advantageous in this respect.

## FEEDING

Feeding any plant is always a matter for great discussion. It must be remembered that the natural habitat of a plant will determine the perfect type of feeding programme to adopt. This is most important regarding the *Pelargonium*. Fortunately they are quite tolerant of abuse and will accept treatments foreign to their true requirements. To produce a plant that will live out its expected natural life-span (and this can be many years), natural methods must be adopted as near as possible, in the use of vital growing components like compost, watering, light level and feeding. It may well be that you are quite happy with the results gained or perhaps do not wish your plants to survive for years — if exhibiting and showing it is uncommon to keep plants for long periods,

*Fig 50 P.cordifolium has heart-shaped leaves often with an outline in red. It is a spreading plant that does not grow too tall.*

bear in mind that the areas of the wild where the majority of pelargoniums grow have intense light levels for most or all of the year and are mainly sandy or stony lands, with very little humus, with minimal or intermittent rainfall or open to early morning dews and sea mists. Therefore, watering should be minimal, sand and drainage should be added to the loam-based compost and mild general liquid type of feed should be used. The rate of feed and the way the feed is given should also be a little different. It is important to remember that pelargoniums like a regular, weak feed. This can be achieved by feeding with a half-strength solution at each watering during the growing season, and at a quarter-strength at other times. The quarter-strength formula should be always used on Miniature types. The types of proprietary feeds on the market are varied, since they are all formulated to do specific jobs – some are organic, some are chemical-based. It is advisable to keep it simple and only acquire a maximum of three or four different feeds or fertilisers. You should have an 'everyday' fertiliser that will be termed as a general or balanced fertiliser, one to give the plants a change now and again and a couple to use for specific purposes, such as to ripen growth and encourage flowering, or to promote good foliage or root growth.

It can be very confusing for the amateur to be confronted by rows and rows of different strengths, makes and forms of feed additives on a visit to the garden centre or nursery, so keep a record of the success rate and the ease with which fertilisers can be administered. A liquid feed is preferred, but has to be made up and mixed with powdered types. Mix the feed with a quantity of warm water·to dissolve the fertiliser, before making it up to the required quantity and use it up that day or even during the same watering. Never leave unused feeds, insecticides, herbicides, or any chemical or horticultural preparation ready mixed, as it is easy to forget and use the watering can another day with possibly disastrous results.

usually a plant of two or three years will not be ideal for further show work. To produce a top quality show plant, a strict feeding and training programme has to be kept to and often a peat-based compost, together with strong feeding is undertaken, because plants grown in a peat-based compost (which is really an unnatural medium for a pelargonium), will grow away very strongly. This medium produces a larger plant in a faster time than conventional methods, so the plant will not survive for the average life-span of the variety or type.

At this point in the book, a natural, basic cultivation programme is being evaluated. So,

The golden rules with horticultural preparations are: keep them tightly fastened; in a safe place away from children, inexperienced users, and animals; always read the whole of the manufacturer's data and instructions; and most important, abide by the directions to the letter. The makers have spent millions of pounds on researching the right usage and dosage so don't use more than you are instructed. It would be folly to add 'one for the pot' and you could ruin the whole plant collection as well as possibly harm animals and humans. Most horticultural fertiliser and additive firms publish leaflets about their products, so try to acquire them, they make interesting and instructional reading. There are also pamphlets dealing specifically with pelargoniums, where details of feeding programmes are dealt with comprehensively.

Only feed a healthy and soil-moist plant; the inexperienced will find it tempting to give fertiliser to a plant that appears sickly, but this mode of practice will not cure a sick specimen, far from it in fact. First, you must find out what is causing the plant's incapacity. It could be just a case of starvation, so you need to know which element of the nutrient requirement, or which trace element is deficient. This is a difficult question and one which cannot, as a general rule, be answered until the specimen is inspected for tell-tale signs, and these are usually evident, at first glance of the foliage, at least to an expert. Finally, feeding should not be carried out until about six weeks after potting, with the exception of hanging baskets.

It is worth discussing the three principles of general feeds or fertilisers. Nitrogen, phosphorus and potassium are known by the initials N:P:K. Nitrogen is vital for growth, and will encourage new vigorous growth, but an over-indulgence of nitrogen will produce soft, lush plant growth which can encourage fungal problems. This is due to the thinning of plant cells and the presence of excess liquid in them, as well as a lack of blooms and seed. Phosphorus encourages strong and thick root development. However, over-use of phosphorus can lead to

disease problems as well. A strong, ripe plant growth that will discourage disease entering the tissues will be promoted by the correct balance of potassium. Potassium encourages seed or fruiting and therefore flowers. Over-use can cause abnormal leaf colour and spotting, as well as early maturity and hard wood. If you purchase a balanced fertiliser from a reputable company, these three essential chemicals will be available in their correct amounts. Never mix more than one feed together, as this will cause an imbalance. In fact, never mix any horticultural products together unless the directions on the package say it is perfectly safe to do so. Governments worldwide are now becoming aware of the problems, both to the environment and to the individual, that may be created through the misuse of chemicals and official booklets are now being published. These can be obtained for a small charge from the relevant authority and give the common names, the proprietary names and chemical names for most horticultural products.

As well as the 'big three' (N:P:K), trace elements like magnesium, calcium, copper, iron, manganese, sulphur, and zinc are also vital for plant growth and development, working with and through the 'big three', and some of the trace elements condition the soil or compost. Experience will prove that some fertilisers create a better form of plant than others, due not only to the type or variety of *Pelargonium*, but also to the general husbandry of the grower. So when one type suits both grower and plant it would be wise to class this type as a favourite.

# GREENHOUSES

## Ventilation

The passage of air through a plant will keep the specimen in a lively, fresh state, deter fungal problems and prevent spent petals from becoming lodged in the centre of the plant. Outside, the passage of air should not be too much of a problem, but if leaves are large and plants stocky and thickly furnished with leaves it may be necessary to remove a few of the inner ones to create a through passage of air. In an enclosed area like a greenhouse or conservatory, a buoyant atmosphere is not easily obtained. It is not always practicable or possible to leave doors open at all times and it is in the winter, when it is too cold for doors to be left open, that good ventilation and air circulation is important. The installation of a small, air-circulating fan is a useful piece of apparatus in the greenhouse or conservatory after automatic windows or louvres have been fitted. The idea of leaving a door open in summer is admirable, but ensure the door is fastened back securely to counter any gust of wind. A small wire mesh gate or door may also be required if animals and birds are likely to frequent the garden and greenhouse.

Sliding doors are much more sensible in a greenhouse than normal hinged types, as they can be opened without the use of a free hand and take up less space when open and cannot slam, thus saving accidental broken glass. Air ionisers are also becoming a popular addition, these electric devices create an atmosphere similar to alpine conditions (remember that in the wild, pelargoniums enjoy an open habitat).

## Heat and Light

Lights are an asset and encourage work to be carried out on dark evenings. Heating will have to be provided if the plants are to be kept in the glasshouse through the winter months and this may be by solid fuel, gas or electricity. There are many types and models on the market which should be evaluated carefully together with your financial and material resources. (Remember that all electrical and permanently-fixed appliances should only be fitted by a qualified engineer.) Conservatories may be heated by an extension of the house heating system. Heated propagators or heated cables for benching are a luxury, but essential if

any propagating is planned during the colder months. If a heater is placed under a bench it may also be used as a gently-heated propagating area.

## Types and Styles

Greenhouses and conservatories are too numerous in style and design to evaluate here. Timber structures are better than metal for plants, because the temperature is more even in all weathers, they also look more natural and are quieter too. Modern techniques of timber construction and preservation are now so advanced that many firms guarantee their products for many years, advising only an annual coat of preservative. Complete full-sized panes of glass will give better light and eradicate the grimy strip that occurs with small, overlapping panes, but replacing large panes of glass will be more expensive. Depending on individual preference a half-wall or one wall of

Fig 51 The National Pelargonium Collection at Fibrex Nurseries.

brick may be built, which will usually keep the temperature warmer and gives extra scope when designing the interior. Ideally, a greenhouse or conservatory should be sited with the longest side running in a south to north situation, but, of course, this is not always possible.

Staging must be planned to fit in as much usable bench space as possible, with at least one gangway of a suitable and practical size. It is also a bonus to have an area without staging, so that tall plants can be grown on a floor bed and allowed to travel into the roof space. Do watch for your tall specimens dropping petals and so on onto plants below and that they do not grow across the roof glass and keep out all important light as well as making glass cleaning awkward. Timber slats will allow air and surplus water to pass through and a bench frame covered with corrugated, transparent plastic will allow water to drain, reasonable air circulation and the area underneath to be used for plants requiring some shade and shelter or to store pelargoniums in a dormant state. If the greenhouse has glass to the floor it may be possible to house plants underneath at all times, but take care that plant debris or compost does not fall through from the benches and cause damage to the plants below. Some benching is of solid design and intended to be covered with sand or a similar material, but these solid benches are not ideal for growing pelargoniums, as they are usually constructed of metal, creating a cold contact for the plant.

The floor itself can be constructed from any clean and suitable material such as cinder, bricks or concrete (although this is cold to the feet) or a wooden slatted duck-board floor, if .long periods of standing are envisaged. Beds in the floor are useful, as are areas where larger, heavy pots can stand, but it is a good idea to add a layer of gravel on any non-porous standing area so that pots can drain properly. Any soil at floor level must be thoroughly sterile before use, and if the soil is in contact with the outside garden soil it must be sterilised from time to time as well as a watch kept for pests.

Most importantly never overcrowd a greenhouse! Arrange pots neatly and alternately in rows on the benching, giving each one plenty of space and at no time allowing a plant to touch its neighbour, remembering that plants will need more space as they grow. Sufficient light around each plant is vital to its health and even growth, so turn plants by one-fifth of the pot's circumference each time they are turned. A quarter turn is not ideal, because an odd amount of turning gives an even chance of light to each part of the plant. This is where another use of plant labels comes in, as if all pots are turned by the same amount and in the same direction, all the labels will be in the same place. When a picking-over regime is carried out, it will be easy to see where a plant has been if the pots are also turned simultaneously.

## Shading

The provision of some form of shading is advisable and there are many types on the market from permanent painted green or white emulsion, removed by dusting at the beginning of the winter period, to roller blinds or sheets of perforated green plastic than can be bought by the yard. The favoured type, particularly in Britain, is the blind or plastic kind which may be put up to the glass on the inside, or preferably the outside of the glass structure and removed during periods of dull weather. Another plus for a timber greenhouse is that you can screw in apparatus or pin up shading and so on. Clear plastic or two layers of plastic sheeting with bubbles of air trapped between, used as an insulation, can also be fitted easily and manufacturers of metal greenhouses have produced various fittings that make fixing sheeting materials on the inside of the metal structure possible. The sheeting will undoubtedly create a damper atmosphere in the greenhouse and condensation can drip on to plants causing problems related to the rotting of foliage, so it is preferable if a structure is made so that the sheeting can be fitted outside the

from one side

from above

even light from all around and above

This plant has a long lanky growth.

The plant is leaning as the leaves strain towards the source of light and it has long lanky petioles.

A stocky plant which is well clad in foliage.

Fig 52 The effect of light.

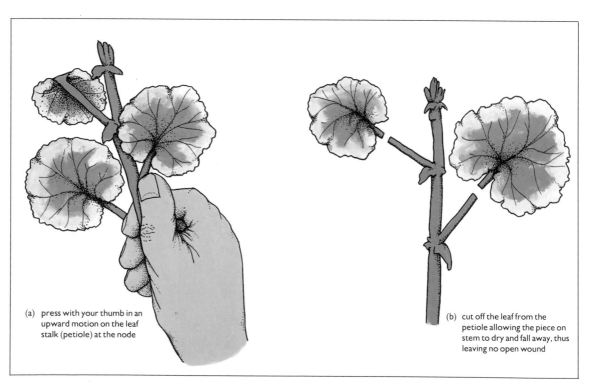

(a) press with your thumb in an upward motion on the leaf stalk (petiole) at the node

(b) cut off the leaf from the petiole allowing the piece on stem to dry and fall away, thus leaving no open wound

Fig 53 Methods of leaf removal recommended, especially when the weather is cold, damp or still.

greenhouse or conservatory. Another problem with this type of protection is the loss of light to the plants shielded by the sheeting, so you must decide whether it is better to save a little heat, or to create a good light and as dry an atmosphere as possible for the *Pelargonium*.

## Good Management

Cleanliness in the glasshouse is very important, as the greenhouse or conservatory is a man-made environment, controlled mainly by the grower. To own a greenhouse or similar structure enlarges your growing potential enormously, enabling plants to be grown in nearly ideal surroundings and in immaculate condition away from the ravages of the weather. In return for good management, this branch of horticulture will give tremendous scope and satisfaction as well as repayment for one's efforts.

## TRAINING YOUR PLANTS

At some stage in their growth some of the plants in your collection will be in need of training to keep them in a neat shape or to encourage general growth or blooms at a specific time. Some cultivars rarely have to undergo this treatment. Terms for this treatment include 'pruning', 'pinching out' and 'dis-budding' and all these three operations are used for different reasons and effects, and have different methods of application.

To prune a plant when it has simply got out of control is simple, but requires a good, long look at the plant before the task is carried out. With a clean, sharp knife make a slanted cut through the stem directly above the node, which should show a forming growth bud, this will then grow into a new flowering shoot and cover the gap left. It is important that the whole plant is evenly treated in this way, keeping a good balance and form and encouraging further balanced growth. If the plant is in good condition,

the pieces may be used as cutting material. If the stem is old, it may be necessary to use secateurs, particularly with Regals, some Species and Uniques. It is better to begin minimal pruning before the plant becomes too old, as old wood may not produce new growth buds and if the stem is thick and old the larger wound may not heal satisfactorily. Take out old wood on larger, old specimens in the same way. If pruning is carried out, new flower buds will not develop for ten to fifteen weeks, depending on their type and variety.

Pinching out, or 'stopping' as it is sometimes called, is carried out to create a well-shaped and many-stemmed plant. It is often done with the forefinger and thumbnail, but this might be a bit clumsy, so use the tip of a very pointed knife, a pair of pointed scissors or a pointed stick to nip or flick out the growing tip of each stem, and this will ensure as little damage and scarring as possible. Pinching out should be done often during the growing period to ensure a well-balanced and stocky plant. Sometimes part of the plant, or perhaps one branch, will grow faster than the rest and pinching out will help to keep this shoot in trim. Pinching should terminate between ten and twelve weeks before the plant is required to bloom. As a newly-rooted cutting is potted up the first stop should take place. This will ensure that the plant will begin branching. At the end of each stopped branch, a pair of new stems, or branches should usually form, so if stopping is continued regularly, a well-shaped specimen will be achieved.

For exhibition purposes both stopping and dis-budding times are crucial. Dis-budding is done to prevent the plant coming into flower. On exhibition plants this is not carried out after about eight weeks before the show date. Each time a plant flowers it takes a lot of energy out of the plant, so for showing purposes the plants are discouraged from blooming until the last possible date. The first series of flowers are the largest and best, and this is another reason for removing buds. Sometimes when a plant is

Fig 54 A display of Regal Pelargoniums on show at The British Pelargonium and Geranium Society's annual competition.

young it will want to flower, which could harm the plant, so it is dis-budded to let the plant grow strong and well shaped first.

Staking will be required on some plants that are heavy in bloom and growth, or are a bit 'leggy' or tall. Ivies in particular will benefit from being staked to an upward growth pattern and will then take up less room in the greenhouse. On show plants, staking is allowed, but must be unobtrusive and necessary. Use green split canes because they will blend into the plant's colour quite well. Always use clean canes or sticks and it is wise to use new ones for the show bench. Use ties with care. Soft green horticultural string is perhaps the best, but can be tricky to tie in some situations. The use of twists is popular, but never twist them too tight as this could cause the stem to snap or become damaged. Insert the cane firmly into the pot,

avoiding the root system as far as possible. Ease the branch or flower stem to the cane and tie in neatly, cutting off the cane just below the top of the supported branch or stem. Arranging and staking a plant correctly can give the plant an evenly-clothed appearance in both foliage and bloom. Other plant supports are readily available in garden centres, such as plastic, supple cane, or a trellis formation, which would be ideal for use with Ivy-leaved or Unique types, to encourage them to scramble upwards. Canes are invaluable during transportation to shows or other events as a temporary support. Wires fixed to the greenhouse or conservatory wall give a tying-in base for larger or climbing plants as well as providing a hanging capacity for the small hanging pots presently so popular. Larger hanging pots and hanging baskets require a much stronger fixing point.

CHAPTER 9

# Cultivating New Plants

## SEED

*Pelargonium* seed can now be bought from seed houses, nurseries and garden centres. These are a little pricey, perhaps, especially F1 hybrid seed. A packet will usually contain between ten and thirty seeds, depending on their type and variety. The seeds will have been removed from their outer coat and will be tan-brown in colour or sometimes a fungicide is dusted over the seeds which will change their outward appearance. Always wash your hands after handling seeds dusted with a fungicide.

If your own plants produce seed, they should be removed as soon as they seem ripe. This ripeness will be evident in fairly dry conditions when the feathery appendage, or awn, begins to furl and the seed curls upwards towards the tip of the style, or central seed-carrying column. Take the whole structure from the plant and place in a paper bag to dry off. Sowing the seed as soon as it is harvested will give better germination results, but if this is impossible, store the seed still in its casing in a cool (not cold), dry, dark place until required. Self-gathered seed or seed not processed professionally is more naturally sown with its awn attached, but this is not imperative. Fill clean pots or trays with a well-aerated seed compost which has been mixed thoroughly with about one-half of horticultural sand, fine Perlite or fine Fullasorb, and press down lightly and evenly when the pot or tray is three-quarters full. Sift the remaining compost to fill the pot and place

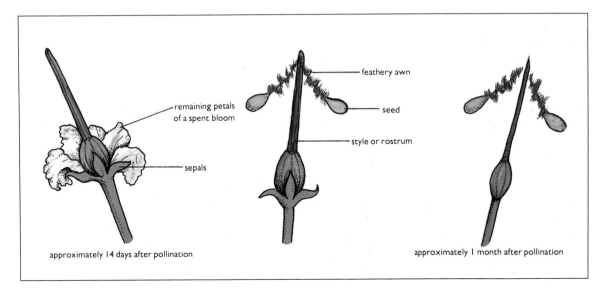

remaining petals of a spent bloom

sepals

feathery awn

seed

style or rostrum

approximately 14 days after pollination

approximately 1 month after pollination

*Fig 55* Pelargonium *seed formation and dispersal.*

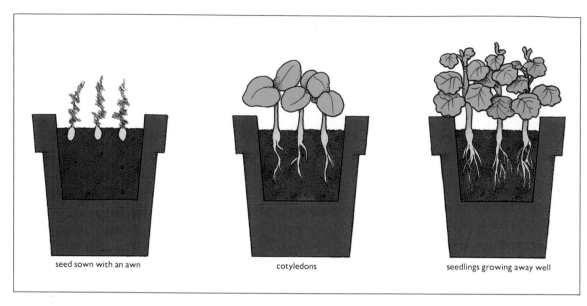

seed sown with an awn          cotyledons          seedlings growing away well

Fig 56 From seed to seedling, ready to be pricked out.

in a reservoir of water, to which a fungicide has been added, to protect the seedlings from damping off problems. Drain well and press the seed point end down into the compost, so that the awn is protruding and able to corkscrew down into the compost when humidity dictates, burying itself to the correct depth. Do not cover it with further compost. (Contrast with cleaned and processed seed which can be laid on the surface and a light covering of compost sieved over them). Germination will have begun when a small whitish place is visible on the seed, which will soon become larger, a root will emerge and the cotyledons will expand and become green and healthy looking. It is vital at this stage that these are not damaged in any way. Seeds may begin to shoot within hours, days or even, frustratingly, weeks. The average time for F1 hybrid seeds to germinate is seven days, although some species can take years, but these are exceptions to the normal. To stimulate *Pelargonium* germination the soil should be at a temperature of 23–25°C (72–75°F), but slightly differing temperatures will only cause slightly differing germination patterns. Do not

cover the tray with any type of lid, as Pelargoniums do not require darkness to encourage germination. Some people recommend the sowing of seed on to moist tissue or paper towels, and some place the planted seed in an airing cupboard or similar. This is quite acceptable but a careful check is required two or three times each day, and as soon as there are signs of the first seed germinating, they must be brought into the light and weaned into cooler conditions. The earlier seeds are sown and begin to grow away, the sooner they will develop into flowering plants – this is especially true with F1 hybrids. Early January sowings will produce a flowering F1 and F2 hybrid by the summer of that year if attention is paid to light and continuous growing techniques, by constantly potting on when necessary. Other forms grown from seed may take longer, which is very frustrating when the seedlings are the results of a hybridising programme being undertaken. It may take a couple of years to assess the flowers and even longer to assess the quality, stability and habit of the new hybrid. As soon as a pair of true leaves have developed, which will provide the seedling with all the required energy to process nutrients into growth, it should be potted up as explained previously.

# CUTTINGS

Creating a new flowering plant from cuttings is a much quicker way than from seed. This method also ensures the flower colour, habit and stability of the end product. A cutting is taken from a mature plant, called a 'mother plant', and this plant must essentially be healthy.

It is important to be organised, so gather together: the mother plant; a quantity of well-sieved sphagnum moss peat; horticultural sand, Perlite or Fullasorb; label and marker; clean pots or trays; a reservoir containing tepid water (with a fungicide if desired) and a razor-sharp knife. The knife must be scrupulously cleaned with a paper towel dampened in a spirit cleaner or Jeyes Fluid solution and then wiped dry. To be absolutely spotless the bench should also be treated and wiped dry with a disinfectant solution. Mix the peat with equal quantities of any or a mixture of the other ingredients and aerate well by sifting through the fingers. Fill the pots or trays to the top and press down very lightly, then soak them in the water until the surface breaks with moisture and drain them for about an hour. A sprinkling of dry horticultural sharp sand may be sifted over the surface, and this will fall into the holes at the base of the cutting when the cutting is placed into the cutting mix. There has been some evidence that the sharpness of the sand will stimulate the base of the cutting in the action of rooting.

## Stem and Tip Cuttings

Next, choose the plant from which your cuttings are to be removed. It may just be a case of using a young mature plant from which perhaps only one cutting can be taken, or a large old plant which will be destroyed once the cuttings have taken, or plants taken up at the onset of autumn, or finally a stock plant grown especially to use as a mother plant. In some cases, when the time is right to prune a plant, any pieces which are healthy or large enough, may be used as cutting material. It is better to choose a plant that is not in bud or flower because flowering weakens the plant. If it is necessary to take cuttings from a plant in bud or in flower, then the buds should be removed at least a week before, to enable the plant to recover its strength.

Stand the plant on a firm bench or table, take a good look at the plant and decide where to cut. With the razor-sharp knife make a clean, slanted cut just above a node (leaf joint) about 3in (8cm) in length, the more leaf buds showing at the leaf-stalk axil the better. If the cut has torn at all, trim and neaten it, and if necessary dust or pat with a fungicide powder to heal the wound. Look again at the mother plant and neaten where required, as well as making adjustments to the plant's shape if necessary. After all the pieces have been removed from one plant, write a label with the variety, date and any other relevant remarks. Gather together all the detached stem pieces. Remove any dead or dying foliage, buds and blooms, inspect for and deal with any insects that may be lurking, then take off the lower leaves, generally leaving two fairly mature leaves as well as the tip growth. To use the tip for cuttings, carefully make a straight cut below the first node. For simple stem cuttings, the piece of stem below where the tip was removed should be cut straight at a node about 2in (5cm) down the stem.

Other forms of stem cuttings can be taken after experience and success with tip and simple stem cuttings. These are often called 'leaf-axil' or 'inter-nodal' cuttings. If you plan to take cuttings in this way, then the piece removed from the mother plant can be as long as you wish, provided the stem is not too old or covered with a brownish skin or bark. At each

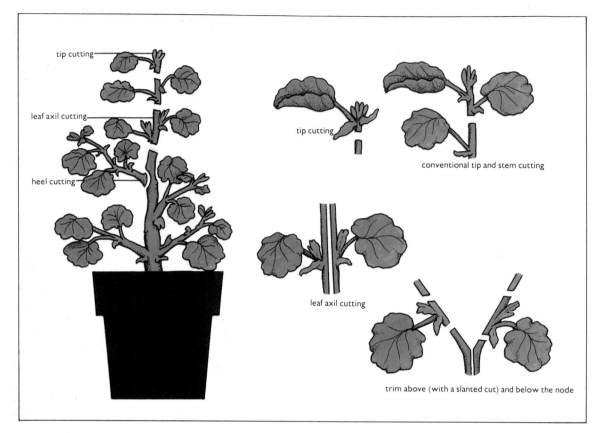

*Fig 57 Simple or conventional stem cuttings (types of stem cutting and where to remove them from the plant).*

node there must be present a sign of, or a developed, leaf-axil bud. Two methods are now open to the propagator. For the first a piece of stem is cut with at least one node in its length, and with about ½in (1cm) above and below the node. Lay the stem piece on to a surface and cut through the total length with a clean, razor-sharp knife, so that you now have two pieces. The other method is to make a slanted top cut in the stem above the node, and a straight cut just below the node, again showing a bud. The reason for making slanted cuts is so that any moisture weeping from the stem or plant will be able to run away rather than sit on top of the open wound and perhaps cause rotting or allow the entry of fungal spores. This method also enables water to drain away when you water the plant as part of its routine.

Where a leaf-bud is growing it is possible to make a type of heel cutting, by slicing through and behind the leaf-bud into the stem, bringing away a heel-shaped piece of stem with the growing bud attached. With any type of stem cutting, the method of 'sticking' the cuttings (as the process is called) into the rooting or cutting medium is exactly the same, it is only the size and shape of the cutting that requires different depths and positions of sticking. With tip cuttings it may be necessary to form a small hole in the compost because the tip cutting will be soft and susceptible to damage from finger pressure.

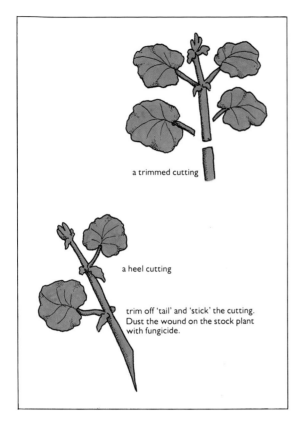

a trimmed cutting

a heel cutting

trim off 'tail' and 'stick' the cutting.
Dust the wound on the stock plant
with fungicide.

*Fig 58 Trimmed cuttings prepared for
planting.*

With larger, simple stem cuttings it is advisable to insert the cutting straight into the mixture, thus ensuring that the cutting fits snugly, with no air pockets at the base, which could lead to rotting off. The inter-nodal cuttings are a little small to handle easily, so carefully press them into the compost at a slant with the leaf-axil bud uppermost, and where two buds are present, slant them away from each other. Leaf-axil cuttings will take longer to root than tip or simple stem cuttings, but will often produce sturdier and more self-branching specimens. Do not cover the cuttings, but place the pots or trays in a warm greenhouse or on a heated bench or propagator tray during the cooler months, at a soil temperature of around 26°C (60°F) – this temperature will suit all. If strong sunlight or intense heat is expected it would be wise to cover the pots or trays with a sheet of newspaper during the first few days. The summer months are better for rooting, but cuttings may be tried all the year round if the correct conditions, including good light and air circulation, are available. Cuttings can also be placed in home-made peat blocks, purchased peat plugs or pots of the type with peat walls – these may be found in strips of smaller pots or in individual pot forms. All peat-based and clay pots must be soaked before use. Cuttings do seem to root quicker when there are a few together in one pot rather than singly. The main drawback with this is that if any fungal problem takes a hold, it will be difficult to control. At all times a careful watch must be made for black-leg, botrytis and other problems, as well as for cuttings which are obviously not going to root, as these must be removed. The time a cutting takes to root varies as a result of temperature, light type and variety, but the fastest will root in four or five days, and the average time during the summer will be ten to fourteen days. It is advisable to pot up as soon as a cutting is rooted, as this will eliminate most root damage and allow the young cutting to 'get away' from an early age. All pelargoniums will root by these last few methods, which are the easiest for the inexperienced to attempt, particularly for Zonal types. However, there are more methods that can be tried.

## Layering

Layering is easy and often does not need any pots of special compost if the plants to be used are growing in the garden. Ivy-leaved varieties and some Scenteds are ideal to try, and others, depending on their stature, may be propagated in such a way. Choose a prostrate branch or stem. Sort out a healthy portion on the under-side, including a leaf node that is fairly near the growing tip. Scrape away a little of the outer skin from the branch or stem; here it may be wise to dust on a little hormone rooting powder.

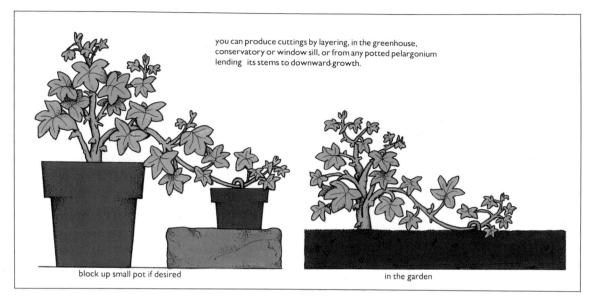

you can produce cuttings by layering, in the greenhouse, conservatory or window sill, or from any potted pelargonium lending its stems to downward growth.

block up small pot if desired

in the garden

Fig 59 Producing cuttings by layering.

Prepare a small area of the soil or alternatively fill a pot with the usual cutting mixture, then lay the branch or stem on to the soil or compost, anchoring it down with a length of wire or a hairpin. Water it lightly to settle the soil or compost around the nodal area. Then leave it to root – this will be from about twenty days. When rooting is obvious, because the node will have developed a new shoot, cut away on the plant side of the new cutting and pot up. Many cuttings can be taken in this way simultaneously, because it does not seem to harm the plant *in situ*, except that flowering could be reduced.

## Root Propagation

New plants can be grown from root cuttings, and Regals and some of the species are more successfully reproduced by these means. Root cuttings from fibrous rooted pelargoniums are the type to choose. These are the most common form of root and comprise strands of fibre structures which transport all the plant's requisites for growth from the soil or water.

Carefully tip the plant out from its pot, and remove a few of the larger roots with a clean knife, and lay them out in such a way that it will be easy to note which end came from the plant, when the narrow end has been cut away. Fill a seed tray or pot with a mixture of John Innes No 2 and sharp sand or other drainage material, mix well, water and drain. Clean off the compost from the roots with the fingers. Trim into 3in (8cm) lengths. Place in a plastic bag to which you have added a small amount of sulphur powder or fungicide powder, and shake it, to dust the roots. Push them, vertically, into pre-made holes, until the tips are still showing on the surface, tap them down to settle the compost, but do not water them. Cover the root cuttings with a layer of dry sand. Place them in or on the propagator at about 18°C–21°C (65°F–70°F) unless the cuttings are taken in the summer, then leave in the greenhouse where the new tip growth should appear after four weeks or so. Pot up in the usual way.

Species having tubers in which they store water and nutrients may be multiplied by

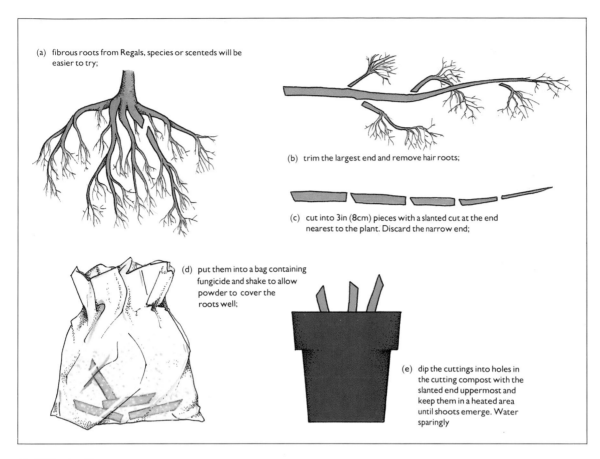

(a) fibrous roots from Regals, species or scenteds will be easier to try;

(b) trim the largest end and remove hair roots;

(c) cut into 3in (8cm) pieces with a slanted cut at the end nearest to the plant. Discard the narrow end;

(d) put them into a bag containing fungicide and shake to allow powder to cover the roots well;

(e) dip the cuttings into holes in the cutting compost with the slanted end uppermost and keep them in a heated area until shoots emerge. Water sparingly

*Fig 60 Root cuttings.*

another method of root propagation. Take the plant very carefully out of its pot and tease out the soil and tubers, some will drop off while others will need to be cut away with care. If the tuber is large enough and there is evidence of an 'eye' or root bud, further multiplication can be undertaken by cutting not quite completely through the tuber. Lay the cut tuber on a saucer of dry sand in a warm, shaded place. The 'eyes' will soon begin to sprout, but leave them a while longer so that the 'eye' is allowed to develop into a shoot. At this point, gently break apart the tuber and pot up as before into an appropriate pot with the correct compost for its type. Leave them in the shade for a day or two, then gradually bring them into full light.

Water the cuttings when required, but this will be minimal.

## Breaking

When your record for 'takes' is satisfactory, try an unconventional way of taking cuttings known as 'breaking'. This method is extremely good with Ivy-leaved types and can be used on others after some experience. All you do is simply break or snap off a cutting at each node, no cutting or trimming is required, and if a clean break is secured, it is possible to acquire with practice a cutting from each leaf joint or node of Ivy-leaved types. This means, of course, that it could be possible to strike dozens of cuttings

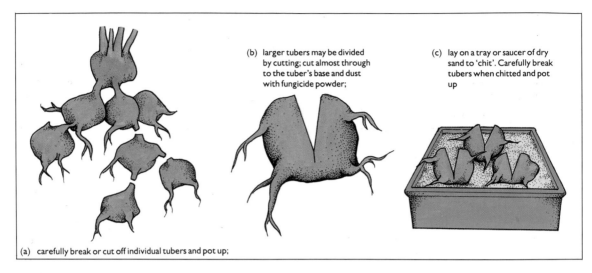

(b) larger tubers may be divided by cutting; cut almost through to the tuber's base and dust with fungicide powder;

(c) lay on a tray or saucer of dry sand to 'chit'. Carefully break tubers when chitted and pot up

(a) carefully break or cut off individual tubers and pot up;

*Fig 61 Root division of tuberous-rooted types.*

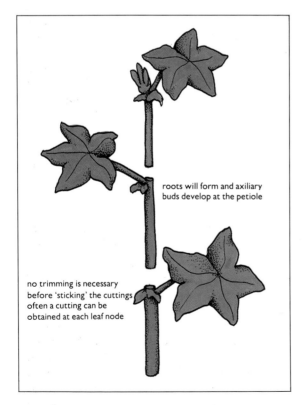

roots will form and axiliary buds develop at the petiole

no trimming is necessary before 'sticking' the cuttings often a cutting can be obtained at each leaf node

*Fig 62 Removing cuttings by the 'breaking' method, the ideal method to use on Ivy-leaved varieties.*

from one plant at one time. Other types of *Pelargonium* can be more difficult to take cuttings using this method than Ivies, and if damage occurs it could be that the plant is not of the correct age or condition to snap when pressure is applied to the node. If the stem just bends then leave it for the time being, as it is not worth spoiling a whole plant.

With all cuttings, wilting must be discouraged if possible. This is initially caused by the plant becoming stressed due to the harsh treatment it has undergone with all the cutting about, handling and so on. Always make sure that the mother plant is well watered the day before cutting material is to be removed. Take as little time as possible (still taking care at every stage) in removing and sticking the cutting. Do not leave it on the bench as the cutting will wilt and the open wound may attract fungal problems. If the foliage is large (as is the case with many varieties), it will be an advantage to cut off half, or perhaps more, of the leaf, even if it is one of the two or so left on the cutting after trimming. Each cutting should be away from its neighbour in the tray and not touching, to allow air to circulate and so prevent the spread of disease.

When a plant does wilt, it is called 'transpiring,' and is a sign of stress which can be likened to a human sweating after a shock and it is just as debilitating for the plant. As a last resort, the plants could be given an overhead spray to counteract this loss of moisture from the leaves. It is a general rule though, that pelargoniums should only be sprayed very occasionally and never during the cooler and duller months.

The use of hormone rooting powder is not usually recommended. Pelargoniums will root readily as a rule, but if you have always used rooting powders or preparations and been successful, then continue to do so. Never dip the cutting into the drum or tub of powder, it is better to tip out a little on to a paper towel and dispose of any left over. In this way each cutting will be fairly safe from fungus and a possibly diseased cutting will not transmit problems to other plants at another propagating session. Powders containing Captan or similar additives are very useful to dab on to open wounds in the mother plant after the cuttings are removed or to dust into a wound caused by accident.

## SPORTS

A chapter on propagation is a good place for an explanation of 'sports'. It has already been said that producing a plant from a cutting ensures that the new plant will be the same as its parent and this statement is true, but for an ever-present exception to the rule. A 'sport' is part of a plant that has developed in an alien manner on a visually perfectly healthy plant. The sport can produce different blooms and leaves from the rest of the plant, in colour, size or formation, or a different general growth habit than the host plant. Normally, the sport will only be on one offshoot from the stem, but if the sport proves to be extra vigorous, it could take over more of the plant area.

Usually, however, the sport is a weak offshoot and if of a markedly different pattern,

colouration and so on than any other variety in existence, it should be propagated to add further to the cultivars available. The grower has to choose one of two methods to ensure this. The first is to cut away the sport and use it as a cutting. Only simple stem propagation should be attempted wherever possible – do not try to be clever with something quite precious! The second option is to remove all normal stems and shoots from the plant to allow the sport to grow on its mother stock until large and strong, then the normal stem cutting can be taken with the possibility of taking some inter-nodal cuttings also. Plants produced from root cuttings will sometimes emerge as sports and a few Golden-leaved types have been introduced this way. Most of the bi-coloured and tri-coloured varieties are sports lacking in chlorophyll. A grower may become excited when different shoots appear on a plant. Unfortunately they will not always be sports, but may be what are known as reversions. When a plant reverts, it will simply be taking on its original form, which is usually its stronger element. It may have been years since the plant originally sported and the true plant may never have been seen by the grower – it can all be very confusing! So, if a sport is produced and cultivated, please check the history of your variety to see if the so-called 'sport' is in fact the plant beginning to revert.

If a grower is fortunate enough to develop a new sport, or indeed any new cultivar by natural means or human methods, it will need a name. The International Registration Authority is the Australian Geranium Society, to whom registration can be sent in the form of a statement regarding the parents, the date of development, detailed description of flower, foliage and habit, the type of *Pelargonium*, whether and by whom it is to be introduced into commerce and the name of the raiser. In the UK, the British Pelargonium and Geranium Society has a Nomenclature Committee to whom application may be sent for a Registration Form. On completion of the form the

*Fig 63 'Hula' which was bred in the USA. A Frances Hartsook hybrid.*

Committee will advise the breeder if the variety is acceptable and the name legitimate. If so, it will be accepted and filed for reference purposes and the Society will then have the right to list the plant if they so wish. When a name is chosen, it must conform with certain standards laid down by the various Nomenclature Authorities around the world, including the proviso that a valid name must have been listed in a dated and distributed document such as a Nursery Catalogue or Plant List. If it is a sport,

then the word 'sport' can be included in the name, or a reference to the plant from which the sport was produced, like 'Golden Bird's Egg' (a sport from 'Bird's Egg'). The name must not already be in use for that particular type, the words 'variety', 'cross' or 'hybrid' cannot be used, but 'variegated' may, if it applies. Names which apply to other plants, such as 'Lilac', cannot be used, but 'Lilac Delight' is all right. Whole words are preferable to abreviations, such as 'Mount Aries' not 'Mt Aries', and title names like 'Mr' or 'Mdm' should also be in full; 'Mister' or 'Madam'. Do not use 'Student', but 'The Student'. Very long words should be avoided, as should names containing more than three words. It is not correct to use words which boast of a plant's attributes, such as 'Brightest and Best'.

It may well be that if the new plant is of high quality and merit, a commercial nurseryman may ask the raiser for some plants or cuttings with a view to listing the plant in future catalogues for sale to the general public. The raiser will never make a fortune and it would be unwise to breed new varieties with the thought of financial prosperity, or else the quality of new varieties would soon begin to lower and second-rate seedlings could flood the market, instead of a judicious selection of only top quality hybrids. Just be content with the thought that no one has ever produced a plant quite like yours. The nursery might ask for a number of plants so that they can build up stocks quickly, or it could be that unrooted cuttings are requested, for the nursery to propagate.

For the amateur, sending anything by a carrier can be troublesome. It is far better to take your specimens to their destination personally, but this is not always possible. Rooted cuttings and small plants can either be left in their pots or taken out and placed in plastic bags with the plastic kept away from the green part of the plant. The day before packing, give the plants a very light watering. This will keep weight to a minimum and the plants will be just moist enough to last the journey which could be three or four days. Try to send them at the beginning of a week to avoid a weekend delay. With string or an elastic band carefully secure around the top of the root so that soil escape will be kept to a minimum and always place the label with the plant. Lay the pots or plants in a strong, shallow container which will allow for a maximum of two rows of plants, because more layers will squash them. Expanded polystyrene seed trays, of the type with sections used for bedding plants, are ideal, and can be placed on top of each other with one plant in each section. Tape round the trays and stick on one self-adhesive label for the address and one for the stamps as ordinary gummed labels will not adhere too well to expanded polystyrene! One or two litre ice-cream boxes also make cheap and effective packaging. Again, use a self-adhesive label and strong sticky tape. Airholes will need to be melted into the base and sides. Mark the parcel 'Fragile – Do Not Delay'. Complete the packing with newspaper as padding so that the plants will not shake about, but do not pack them too tightly.

Unrooted cuttings can be sent in similar containers, and each batch must be labelled. Here, plastic bags can be used to keep the cuttings fresh, but a few pin-holes should be made so that the air inside does not become too damp and stagnant from the moisture of the plant. An excellent way to send unrooted cuttings through the post or by carrier is to dampen a piece of flower-arranging foam, stick the cuttings and labels into the foam and then lay each section in the box without any bags, but just newspaper to pack around the contents. I sent a package of cuttings in this way, which was delayed in transit, and on arrival the condition of the cuttings was excellent, in fact, some of them had begun to root! When you take unrooted cuttings personally to a nursery or to a friend, use flower-arranging foam to keep them in tip-top condition on the journey.

If plants or cuttings are to be sent to another country, by hand or by carrier, you will need to become acquainted with the regulations regarding plant health restrictions. This information may be obtained from a local Ministry of Agriculture office. Please make sure you abide by all the regulations – not only are laws broken by not conforming, but plants will be destroyed if found to be without their phytosanity documents or similar. It is permissible to take plants to some countries without much trouble, while some require the plants to be inspected by a Ministry Official and others

*Fig 64 'Rogue', a Regal variety having red petals with a mahogany blotch. A compact and low-growing plant.*

require all soil-type materials to be completely removed. This can only be done by washing with a fairly fierce stream of water, which unfortunately no plant enjoys! Sending tubers and seeds is much easier, although tubers may have to be Ministry-inspected too. Seeds will have been dried before transporting, so all that is required will be a small, waxy-glazed envelope for the seeds and some type of protection in the form of bubble plastic sheeting or a padded envelope that can be easily purchased. Because of the method of automatic sorting and roller-stamping in most principal postal areas, this type of padding is strongly recommended! Mark the envelope 'Fragile – Please Hand-stamp'. Tubers should be sent dry in a rigid container with packing around each one and a label. You should also advise the recipient to plant the tubers as soon as they arrive, and to water them, to encourage them to grow.

# CHAPTER 10

# Uses of Pelargoniums

The *Pelargonium* is one of the most versatile plants and one of the most commonly grown, and because of the vast colour range and various types of the genus, there are a multitude of uses, both indoors, under glass and outdoors in the frost-free months.

## POT OR HOUSE PLANTS

The most popular use of a *Pelargonium* is as a pot or house plant. Here the Regal Pelargonium reigns supreme and begins the year with a splendid show of trumpet-shaped blooms on shrubby plants, just in time for Mothering Sunday and Easter. Following later in the spring come the Zonal Pelargoniums ('geraniums'), usually as the previous year's plants that have been over-wintered in the nursery and encouraged into early bloom on mature well-branched plants. As a pot plant, the semi-double or double forms are favoured, due to their large flower heads (umbel) and non-shattering petals. Ivy-leaved types are not usually grown as house plants because of their sprawling nature, but training them upright against trellises gives a reasonable pot plant requiring a fair amount of space. In recent years the Miniature and Dwarf Zonal, Miniature and Dwarf Ivy-leaved and Angel types are becoming rightly more popular. The Miniature and Dwarf range will generally bloom for many months during the year, if plenty of even light and extra warmth are provided.

Aromatic-foliaged plants have given a new lease of life to the *Pelargonium* section with the Scented-leaved varieties. They are charming species and cultivars grown primarily for their aromatic foliage, with small to medium blooms, although recent hybridisers have introduced cultivars with large blooms. The shape of the foliage is diverse, and some possess variegated foliage which adds to the attraction of any pot plant. They are also varied in size, ranging from 6ft or more (2m plus), down to compact plants of 4 or 5in (10–13cm). Such plants are at home on the kitchen window-sill and most scented varieties are useful as an alternative to herbs and flavourings, as well as releasing their aroma when the leaves are touched or bruised. The rubbing of the leaves, within reason, will not damage the foliage at all. Remember that all plants grown on a window-sill or in a similar situation should be turned by one-fifth, three or more times a week. See also chapter 8 for all other procedures applicable to the growing of pelargoniums as pot or house plants.

Pelargoniums are happy in pots outside from the end of spring until the signs of the first frost in the autumn. Patio and balcony gardening are fashionable at present, and for those living in flats and apartments, container gardening is a totally new experience to many who have never done any gardening before. Most types of *Pelargonium* will prove perfect. Large pots made of plastic, fibre, stone, terracotta, or concrete are on sale at garden centres and nurseries, as well as hardware stores and do-it-yourself outlets. The size of the pots will obviously determine how many plants are to be included in the arrangement. Pelargoniums will not object to being pot-bound so long as there is adequate air circulation as well as water and feed. Other plants such as annuals can be

*Fig 65 Some of the many kinds of ornamental containers available.*

mixed in the planting for extra colour, but it is wise to plant together all those plants with similar tastes in compost, feeds and amounts of water as well as light requirements. It is a mistake to plant pelargoniums with fuchsias for example, because they have different growth habits, but petunias do go well with them.

Depending on the type of tub, patio pot or large pot used, some mesh or even a square cut from a pair of old tights should be laid over the drainage hole and then a layer of gravel or crock placed in the base of the pot. Some plastic urns or pots do not have holes cut, but have an indentation ready for them to be made – it is essential that all pots used outside have drainage holes. When using clay or fibre pots,

soak them for an hour or two to moisten the shell. Compost should be a soil-based John Innes No 3 type, this is stronger than the compost used for potted plants, but as the weather will affect the growing conditions and leach the fertiliser through the pot or urn, a stronger mix is suitable. Plant up in the usual way by removing a portion of compost to situate the root-ball; a drop of water into the hole will assist the root system to grow immediately. Carefully place the compost around the plant and gently pat it down to settle the compost. It is likely that the plants will be in bloom when planting up tubs and so on, for summer displays. Normally they should not be potted up or potted on while in bloom, but

84

*Fig 66 Pelargoniums used to brighten up 'patio living'.*

in this situation, if a pot the same size as the one containing the plant is used as a mould and the compost pressed around it before it is removed, the plant added and watered in, then hardly any setback will occur. Place a layer of grit or gravel on the surface to prevent rain splashing and spoiling the flowers and leaves as well as to deter slugs and snails. It also keeps the roots cool and gives the whole pot a pleasant appearance. The watering of outside planters will depend on the rainfall and wind as well as the sun and temperature, but where possible allow the tub to just dry out and then give it a good watering. Extra feeding is necessary and may be given twice a week if rain washes nutrients out. A good general feed made up in liquid form is best. Inspect the plant for any weather damage that can cause many fungal problems as well as slugs and snails and other

insect pests. Take off dead and dying flowers and leaves regularly. Staking or some support will sometimes be needed; this can be carried out in the same way as for potted plants, but take care to protect the tops of any protruding canes.

## WINDOW-BOXES

Window-boxes and troughs should be planted up in the same fashion. Always ensure that brackets for window-boxes are more than adequate to carry the weight of the filled trough, which can be quite heavy by the time compost, plants and water are in place. Choose plants carefully, especially if the window-box is sited in a window space that is used. Plants of small stature such as Miniatures and Dwarfs and

Fig 67 Cascade types tumbling from a balcony window-box.

some of the small-growing Scented-leaved varieties and trailing Ivy-leaved types will be ideal. A window-box situated in the window of a gardenless apartment planted with the Scented-leaved forms that can be used in cookery, together with culinary herbs, will provide interest throughout the summer.

## BEDDING SUBJECTS

Many gardens have an area of 'bedding' which is newly planted each season to give an ever-changing splash of colour throughout the year. Following the removal of the previous occupants of the bed, the soil should be weeded, forked over and a sprinkling of granular balanced fertiliser raked in. Any soil-borne troubles observed or suspected must be eradicated. If possible, the bed should be sited away from overhanging trees, shade caused by buildings or shrubs and so on, and protected from prevailing winds. Plan out the planting display on squared paper first, using pelargoniums as the main part or the whole design. In small beds it is worth using the flower colour to accentuate the area. For instance, use paler shades of flowers at the rear of the display if the bed is narrow and the depth of the plot is to be maximised, or use paler shades at each end if the bed needs to look longer. Do not use many different colours or types in one bed as this will create a messy looking scheme. It is much more striking if a simple, but bold plan is adopted.

Use 'dot plants' to heighten and add interest; these can be pelargoniums grown as semi or full standards, or pots and baskets sitting on pedestal-type structures, or Ivy-leaved varieties grown up canes or small trellises. All forms of *Pelargonium* may be used outdoors during the summer, but Regals are not too happy with the effects of the British weather on their delicate blooms, and will not flower into the late summer period. Basic Zonals and Ornamental-leaved Zonals are the most popular for bedding and some Scenteds will provide interest both as dot plants and, the smaller varieties, as edging plants. Miniatures and Dwarfs are ideal in small beds or as edgings and also on the rockery. On large rockeries, the Ivy-leaved varieties will be happy and look attractive, they may also be used as

ground cover in beds. If plants are to be bought rather than grown from your own stock, choose those varieties with stiff, strong foliage which will weather much better as rain runs off shiny foliage more easily than soft velvety leaves. This will be an expensive outlay and to buy or raise F1 varieties or F2s will be more economical. The F1s will give a uniform performance, but may not begin to flower until mid to late summer. Picking over will extend the flowering season as well as prevent pests and diseases in the bed.

At the first hint of frost in the autumn, plants must be taken into a sheltered and frost-free place to over-winter. The lifting of pelargoniums is made easier if the plants are potted before the bedding time and then both the

*Fig 68 'Mangle's Variegated' has a single flower of bright red.*

plant and pot sunk into the bed, which will also keep the roots from running riot into rich garden soil, thus encouraging blooms rather than rich, lush foliage. During the summer the plants will require a high potash feed at weekly intervals to keep the blooms coming.

## STANDARDS

From time to time you may wish to create an unusual display for the garden using a *Pelargonium* as the star turn. Standard trained plants are well known and easy to achieve. For home and garden use, the bare stem may be of any reasonable, practical height, but remember that the end product will need to be sited out of strong winds to prevent the top-heavy pot from falling over and the heavy head of growth from becoming damaged, or the stem breaking in the wind. Choose a new cutting that has not yet been stopped and shows an unwillingness to self-branch – some types and varieties show this characteristic more than others. Abandon the next size of pot and pot into a large one. Insert a cane and make a protective tip. Tie in the stem as the plant grows, but take care not to tie it too tightly as it will be necessary to loosen the ties as the stem develops. The stem should be kept as straight as possible. Erratic feeding will encourage erratic growth and the stem will grow unevenly. The leaves should be left on at this stage, but any branches must be nipped or rubbed out as soon as the shoots are visible as buds. The leaves will fall off naturally, usually when the head is first formed, or they may be carefully removed. When the stem has reached the required height, allow two or more branches to develop as evenly as possible on the stem, then nip or pinch out the tip of the stem. The branches now form the top growth or head and should be rigorously pinched back, all at the same time, to create a balanced, bushy, compact head. All flower buds should also be removed until ten or twelve weeks before the standard or half standard is required

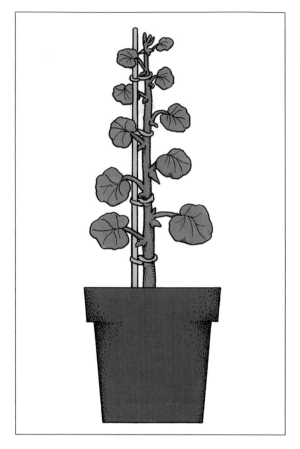

*Fig 69 At the first stage of developing a standard plant, only remove any side shoots and buds which appear on the stem.*

to come into flower. It will take a season and a half to complete the building of a good standard plant and during this time, a general, regular feeding programme is carried out. The stake or cane will need to be left in.

Sometimes Ivy-leaved varieties are trained as upright specimens either as single stemmed standards or as multi-stemmed, these can look very attractive due to the cascading quality of the final top growth. When placing the pots of either full, half or quarter standards into the garden, it is a good idea to hammer an extra stake or strong cane right through the pot's base and into the garden soil to help ensure that the specimen is as secure as possible in its

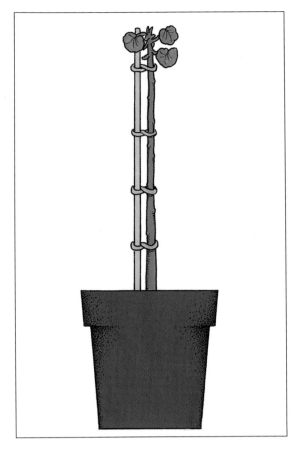

Fig 70 At the second stage of developing a standard plant when the stem is at the required height, remove the tip and allow the shoots to develop at the top of the stem. These shoots will be the basis or the 'head'. Do not forget to loosen the ties.

Fig 71 At the third stage of developing a standard plant, continue pinching out until a bushy, well-balanced 'head' is formed, before allowing any blooms. Loosen the ties where necessary and check that the cane is still strong, especially in the compost.

situation. Over-wintering a plant such as this is a problem, it must be housed in a frost-free and preferably a warm place, to allow the plant to just tick over during the winter months. If the plant can only be housed in a frost-free area, then the main stem will need to be protected as a precautionary measure. The ideal way to cope with this is to buy a length of foam pipe insulation, shaped as a length of pipe with a ready-made slit, which can be opened up and slipped on to the plant's stem. Cut back the branches on the head to reduce the size and also reduce watering. Inspect for any damage,

especially to the main stem, before covering with the foam tubing. Any plants taken from an outdoor site must be expected to harbour insects, slugs and snails and appropriate action must be taken before the rest of the plants in the greenhouse are affected.

Another unusual and attractive structure can be created that does not take up a great deal of space and can stand on the patio or in the garden – a column of Ivy-leaved Pelargoniums. This will give a beautiful display throughout the

Fig 72 An interesting method of displaying trailing types; the variety used is 'Pink Mini Cascade' synonym 'Rose Mini Cascade'.

summer as a centrepiece in a bed; on the balcony or patio. Acquire a length of squared plastic mesh, the type sold as climbing plant and clematis support. The green or brown colour is more natural. Fasten the longest edges securely by over-sowing or whipping wire through the squares along the length of the piece, thus making a cylinder. The size is up to you, but do not make it too large or too tall and narrow or it will be difficult to make the cylinder stable. A maximum size of about 14in (35cm) in diameter and 3–4ft (100–130cm) high will be practical in a small garden, but much smaller ones are just as good. In soft ground you must insert three or four canes through the whole display to ensure it will stand squarely on the bed. Line this with a plastic dustbin liner. Make holes in the bottom for drainage. Fill it with a soil-based compost, at the same time inserting a piece of pipe, in which holes have been drilled at intervals to assist in the watering, through the centre. Cut out small holes in the sides of the plastic liner for the small plants. Small-leaved Ivy-leaved types are ideal, cascading over and down the sides making an attractive floriferous column. Water through the pipe, feed and dead-head them regularly.

## HANGING BASKETS

Hanging baskets are an age-old addition to a garden, and will adorn smaller modern homes. It is very important to choose the position of a hanging pot or basket carefully before going out to purchase one. Is the basket to be hanging over a doorway? In this case it will need to be fitted with a drip-tray. Is it likely to be in a constant wind? If so perhaps a solid type which would not dry out so quickly will be better. Baskets should never be hung in a draught or in a known windy situation, neither should they be placed in a corner. Make sure the basket is high enough to prevent annoyance, but low enough to be viewed easily. A basket of pelargoniums must have light and although they enjoy the sun, do not place it in an exceptionally hot spot because the basket cannot be moved often once it is in position. How much space is available? Maybe the new hanging pot could be accommodated more sensibly.

There are many sizes of baskets and pots on the market, so it should be easy to find one to suit. Some are constructed of open mesh wire which may be covered in plastic of usually green or brown. Cast iron or similar metals are used in more decorative varieties like an animal manger or hay basket. Slatted timber and peat mache baskets are also available. Many types are of solid or mesh plastic in various colours and most are available with a drip-tray that clips on to the pot or basket, or is a permanent fixture. There are even baskets constructed in tiers. Sizes range from 4in (10cm) for a hanging pot to 20in (50cm) for a full-sized professional basket. Baskets come in mainly two shapes; round or half round. Round baskets are mostly semi-spherical (these are usually used in shows), but some have flat bases which can be easier when planting up. The half round types are also sometimes found with flat bases. These half baskets are for mounting directly on to a wall or fence and so on, without the need for a bracket. Pick the type and size to suit your pocket as well as your chosen situation, remembering that a large basket will cost more to fill. Take notice of the metal chain. Is it rust-proof and can it be removed? Is it strong enough?

The next requirement is a bracket – and also make sure that the wall or wherever it is to be fixed is sound. A large basket will be very weighty when filled, especially when freshly watered or swinging in the wind, so the bracket chosen must be capable of taking this weight. The size of the top arm of the bracket, from where the basket will hang, should be at least equal to the basket's width, which will allow for the plants to spill over the sides with a margin of room between the wall so that in strong winds the plants or basket will not be buffetted against the building. Good strong wall plugs and lengthy screws must be used to fix the bracket to the wall or timber.

Baskets of wire or mesh will require a lining to contain the compost as well as to keep the roots cool. Many preformed liners are available, but many do not fit baskets properly and some are constructed from plastic, which are hard and sharp on the edge and will damage overhanging stems. Paper, peat and card fibre types must be soaked first, as must the new type made from coconut fibre. Foam sponge in neutral colours, split for the basket, is quite good. Plastic or polythene sheeting is often used, but does not look pleasant and cannot soak up moisture to release into the basket in dry conditions; however, it is cheap, and can be cut from old compost bags. By far the best medium for lining a basket is sphagnum moss which can either be purchased, or if the gardener is lucky, can be acquired from the wild. The one disadvantage that can easily be overcome is the possibility of insects and slugs and so on being present. Always sprinkle a granular insecticide and slug guard on to the top of the basket when it is completed. Other cheap liners can be made from old tights, turves, sacking and carpets made from natural fibres. Live lining is a challenge and can look very attractive too: 'Baby's Tears' (*Helxine soleirolii*), *Ajuga reptans*, mossy saxifrages and many other hardy carpeting plants can be experimented with.

Watering is the great drawback with baskets. Most usually goes over the edge or on the waterer! Some pump-like devices are on sale for the watering of high baskets and pots. A similar piece of apparatus can be made from a

Fig 73 'Flakey', a Miniature variegated Ivy-leaved variety in a hanging pot.

washing-up liquid bottle, a length of small bore plastic tubing (such as that used by home wine makers or aquarium keepers and available from those outlets) and a piece of wire which is inserted through the tubing so that the tubing may be bent into a hook and adjusted to suit. The wire and tubing is pushed through an enlarged hole in the bottle top and when filled with water and squeezed it will be a useful, cheap aid in watering baskets. A watering can with a small nozzle is better although it does take time to water well. Baskets, especially mesh types, must be watered at least daily until the water runs through and drains away, and on hot sunny days you may need to do it twice. Feeding at half dosage which is mixed with the water, must also be carried out daily, as often water and feed will drain through too quickly, so that the feed is not used by the plants. A

simple technique is to freeze a feed solution in an ice tray specially kept and well labelled for the purpose; the ice cubes may then be placed on the compost surface and allowed to melt, thus seeping slowly into the basket (if there are children around this is not advised). A small, empty flower pot sunk into the centre of the top of the basket can be filled with water and will empty fairly slowly into the compost. If a basket does become too dry then dunk the basket for an hour or so in a bowl of water, and allow it to drain before re-hanging.

## Making Up

To make up a basket, gather everything you need together: compost; plants; lining material; a small piece of plastic sheet or a plastic plant saucer; the basket; and a larger flower pot or bucket. Stand the large pot or bucket on a table or bench and place the basket into the top to stop round-based baskets from moving. Take off at least one of the chains carefully, doing this will assist when the basket is full and the chains have to be lifted up and over the plants ready to be fixed. Select the liner which should have been soaked beforehand if needed, sphagnum moss should be checked for insects and thorns which can be painful as the moss is pressed in to a basket shape. Fill the inside edges of the base of the basket with the moss and lay the saucer or plastic sheeting on top of this to act as a reservoir. If the basket is to be of a mixed kind and include annuals like alyssum, petunias and so on, three or more of these plants can be inserted through the wires in each layer starting at the bottom. Add the compost on to this first layer, which may be of a peat-based type to lessen weight, although a soil-based one will be better for the *Pelargonium* and will absorb moisture easily, especially if the basket accidentally becomes dried out. Add more moss up the basket sides, more compost and another layer of filler plants. This is carried on until the top of the basket is reached.

If the basket is to be exhibited for competition,

92

it is unlikely that the schedule will allow any other plants but pelargoniums. Fill the sides to the top and slightly above, coming above the wire edge with the moss to allow for it to settle. More moss for extra height will ensure that the water will not spill over the edge so readily and also protect the plant stems from rubbing on the wire edge. And so to the top layer. If you wish you can insert the watering pot near the centre. For shows, a plastic sheet liner is sometimes used because it is not so messy to transport. Decide which plants are to go where. Most prefer a basket using only one variety and this is normal for show baskets, but it is up to the individual. Three plants are adequate in a basket up to 12in (30cm) across and some people also like to add one in the centre. The centre plant is usually, but not necessarily, an upright variety.

The Ivy-leaved types are ideal to ramble and trail to their hearts' content, and they will stand a certain amount of training and tying in to disguise the chain and outside of the basket. When planting up anything with more than one plant it is more attractive to use an odd number of main plants; this applies as much to hanging planters as to ground level displays. A very large basket may contain many plants, but the more plants you have growing in a confined space, the more watering and feeding will be necessary. The plants used should really be in bloom and of a semi-mature to mature state to give an instant display.

Use an empty pot to make a 'mould' in the compost of the larger pot and water the hole. When the basket is completed, water the top of the compost, taking special care to water round each main plant. Cover the top of the

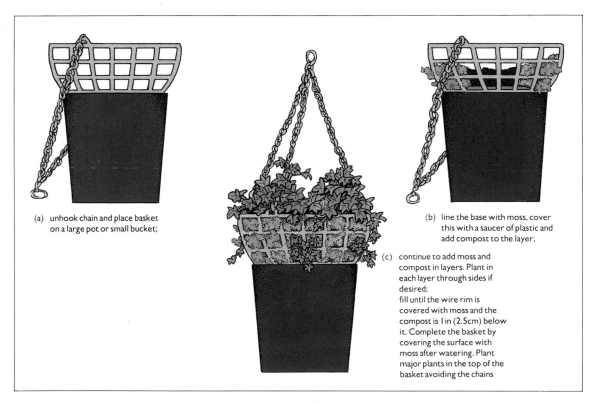

(a) unhook chain and place basket on a large pot or small bucket;

(b) line the base with moss, cover this with a saucer of plastic and add compost to the layer;

(c) continue to add moss and compost in layers. Plant in each layer through sides if desired;
fill until the wire rim is covered with moss and the compost is 1in (2.5cm) below it. Complete the basket by covering the surface with moss after watering. Plant major plants in the top of the basket avoiding the chains

*Fig 74 Planting a hanging basket.*

basket with a layer of moss and a few slug pellets. Solid baskets, which will only be planted in the top, will also look more finished with a moss layer and the moss helps to keep the plants' roots cool as well as conserve moisture. When all is finished, sink the basket into a large receptacle filled with tepid water, leave for an hour to complete a thorough soaking, then drain it well before hanging. When hanging large and heavy baskets, stand on safe steps or similar and if possible have an assistant – don't take chances as newly watered and planted baskets are very heavy.

## Hanging Pots

Smaller hanging pots are useful in a greenhouse or conservatory situation as well as outdoors. Most have a clip-on base tray to minimise drips, which is most welcome in the greenhouse or conservatory where wet, slippery floors should be avoided. It is possible to buy the plastic hangers as a separate item and these will fit most plastic pots with a strong roll to the rim. There are hanging pots on the market of solid plastic and in various colours, and if you choose terracotta, green or black, it will not detract from the beauty of the plants. Wooden slatted pots are reasonably easy to buy, as orchid growers use them extensively. You can also buy the strong plastic mesh pots sold for use in pond plantings. Both these types of pot will need a layer of moss in the inside. Plants do seem to prefer mesh-type hanging containers. If these containers are situated in the greenhouse or conservatory or perhaps a glass porchway, more watering will be required, and take care that the plants do not become scorched from the sun if they are high in the roof space and near to the glass. Using hanging pots and small baskets in this situation can increase your plant growing area greatly and give most subjects the space to trail and scramble that may not be possible when standing on benching. They represent an ideal way to add simultaneously to your collection and to the attraction of your home.

Fig 75 An attractively variegated form of 'Clorinda', known as 'Golden Clorinda'.

## OTHER USES

You can also dry the leaves of non-sticky Scented-leaved Pelargoniums, crush them and add them to dry petals of scented flowers, such as carnations and roses. Add to these a mixture of spices and a fixer of orris root and after a spell to mature, the mixture will delightfully perfume a room, scented pillow or sachets filled with the pot-pourri. Petals or complete heads of *Pelargonium* flowers can also be dried in sand or Borax to add colour to pot-pourri bowls. The complete heads, when dry, may be wired and used in dried flower arrangements.

It is a simple task to make a flower press, or even use a heavy book to press the petals for use in pressed flower portraits or smaller items

Fig 76 A floral arrangement using pelargoniums.

like bookmarks and greetings cards. The pressed petals may also be affixed to candles with the back of a warm spoon. Carefully rub the spoon over the candle, where the mounting is to be, then add the petals and give a final rub over with the warm spoon to fix the motif to make a special but inexpensive gift. And finally, a drop of 'geranium' oil on the wick will make a simple, scented candle.

The leaves of the Fruit- and Flowered-scented varieties can be infused and the resulting 'geranium waters' used as the basis for many cosmetic and toilet preparations. The Fruit, Flower, Spice and Herb-scented types can be used in the kitchen for unusual flavourings in both savoury and sweet dishes, as well as in baking and confectionery. A few petals will also add interest to fruit salad.

Pelargoniums are marvellous for flower arranging. They will last for weeks in clean water and the colours and various forms available make interesting centrepieces for any table or large arrangement. The leaves of Scented-leaved varieties add to the charm. Try to pick the blooms before the sap has begun to rise, early in the day, and place them up to the flower in cold water for an hour before cutting and using. The semi-double and double forms will last better in water because the petals will not shed so quickly. Do use the foliage too, especially from Ornamental varieties and sprigs of the more petite varieties.

Remember to ensure that the plants from which any part is to be taken for recipes, toiletries or cosmetics, and so on, have not been sprayed with any kind of horticultural chemical or similar and at least are not used inside the manufacturer's time lapse stated on the preparation. Wash all leaves and blooms before use.

CHAPTER 11

# Pests, Diseases and Disorders

In any horticultural book, the chapter on pests, diseases and disorders is daunting for the beginner. The lists seem endless and the descriptions horrific and some would-be *Pelargonium* enthusiasts could even be put off. This is certainly not the intention. It is unlikely that the plants in your collection will be afflicted with any but the commonest pest or complaint and even more unlikely that any one plant will ever suffer from more than one or two maladies. Some pests and diseases are found in one type of *Pelargonium* and not in others and some varieties are also more prone to certain ailments. Be aware of the danger of using chemicals in the garden and greenhouse – this cannot be emphasised enough. Always keep bottles and packets tightly fastened and in cool, dark storage places, away from children and animals. Do not breathe in any sprays and watch for spray-drift dangers. If the instructions recommend wearing protection then heed the warning. Take note of all instructions and directions. It is wise to keep a notebook to list all your garden products in, together with the instructions and directions written in full, the date of purchase and the price and size of the product. Recording details such as these will prevent overdosing, and so on, if directions become illegible on the bottle or packet label. Never guess the dosage – it is far safer to throw away the unlabelled product.

Many horticultural firms print descriptive leaflets advertising their products, which are useful because the illustrations will help you to identify and control a particular disease or pest. These will be sent to you, usually on receipt of a stamped addressed envelope. All treatments can be classified into either 'organic' – derived from plants or other natural materials; or 'chemical' – generally man-made.

## PESTS

### Ants

Ants find their way into the greenhouse and conservatory, mainly during the spring, and into pots on the patio in the summer, from where they can move an incredible volume of compost and disturb roots. Dusting powders and syrup products are widely available for this only slightly problematical pest.

### Aphids

There are many kinds of aphids, but in the glasshouse, greenfly is the main problem. They will colonise at the tips or on the youngest shoots, sucking the sap and causing the shoots to curl and go yellow and distorted. The residue from their escapades will be found on the upper surface of foliage below the colonisation, as a sticky honeydew. This will become black and dusty in time and is known as honeydew or sooty mould which is a potential harbouring for other fungal problems. The mould can be washed off with a mild solution of soap-based washing-up liquid sprayed on to the white powder on the roots and on the inside of the pot. Their activities will stunt growth and in turn cause the upper parts of the plant to become yellow. (This yellowing should not be confused with the natural yellowing of *Pelargonium* leaves which may appear from time to time.) Drench the compost with an aphid insecticide.

## Blackfly

These are also aphids and are similar in pest value to the greenfly. The same preparations may be used. Smokes for use in killing aphids are available, but should be used with caution. There are systemic insecticides that can be applied, which are then absorbed into the plant cells, and these will destroy the nymphs as soon as they hatch. Some of the sprays that are available, on the other hand, will only touch the adult fly.

Many insects are becoming immune to various insecticides and it would be wise to change the type used from time to time so that the colony does not become accustomed to the same preparation. Aphids have many predators including ladybirds which, in a slight infestation, will help to keep the pest under control during the warmer months. If predators are being used, it will not be wise to use many of the insecticides available for fear of killing them also. There is a problem with heated greenhouses and centrally heated rooms in lowering the size of aphid colonies which is naturally done by normal outdoor conditions during our winter. Look carefully and often for signs of attack and treat at once; the treatment should be continued at regular intervals to catch each brood as it hatches until the problem is overcome. Never use sprays in bright sunshine or last thing at night. Not only will aphids weaken the plant, but they will also encourage the penetration of other disease and fungal problems through the tiny apertures they have made in the plant's tissue.

Fig 77 Aphids can infest a variety of plants including pelargoniums.

leaves, which may also help to kill off the greenfly, but there are many other products available to do this task. Recently insecticidal soaps have been introduced to the market, to be used as sprays to combat aphids. The greenfly will shed its skin from time to time, which can be unsightly and is an ideal place for fungus to survive. The main section of *Pelargonium* to be affected by greenfly are the Ivy-leaved and a few species.

## Root Aphids

These are a problem and can be found when a plant is removed from the pot, appearing as tiny grey to white insects with small patches of

Fig 78 An example of the damage a caterpillar can do to a leaf. They are a pest to watch out for.

## Caterpillars

Known to everyone, and detected by the appearance of large or small holes in foliage, depending on the type and size of caterpillar. They are normally found outdoors, but on the odd occasion will creep undetected into the glasshouse. The safest way is to pick them off and destroy them with either your boot or a bucket of water. Often caterpillars cannot be found until nightfall, which is an ideal time for a torch-lit caterpillar safari! They will attack leaves and shoots and because of their incisions will create other problems in the plant tissue. The unsightly droppings should be removed, because they will rot on the leaves in damp weather. There are killers on the market, but usually picking off by hand is sufficient. It could be that the caterpillars on the plants could be the grub stage of some rare butterfly or moth, so if they are not familiar, it is worth finding a reference book on the subject to give you more information on the different species.

## Cats and Dogs, Mice and Birds

These must all be classed as pests from time to time. Fouling and scratching in a neat bed of seedlings or plants is annoying. A bucket of cold water will often do the trick, but there are repellants which can be bought and do a moderately effective job of deterring animals from the garden. Mice will nibble at stems of plants and, if they find their way into the glasshouse, will also nibble tubers. The use of the rather barbaric mousetrap or poison may perhaps be the only answer.

## Cutworms

Cutworms are recognised as a garden pest, but if the floor of the greenhouse has a soil bed or an earth base, it is possible for them to take up residence. In appearance, the worm is not worm-shaped, as one would expect, but more like a short caterpillar of a dull, beige-brown colour. The devastation caused by a cutworm chewing through stems and shoots at ground level is heart-breaking and a new bed of pelargoniums can be ruined overnight. Stamp on any you find while preparing the bed and sprinkle with a granule made for the purpose of killing them before planting.

## Earwigs

Earwigs do not pose a big problem, but will sometimes chew petals, leaving them ragged and unsightly and certainly no good for the show bench.

## Eelworms (*Nematode*)

Roots, stems, tubers and foliage are damaged. It is safer to destroy all affected plants and sterilise the soil, but with diligence the soil may be totally removed and replaced, although the plant might not be too happy about this! Good clean growing conditions, including compost, will mean that eelworm attacks should remain

*Fig 79 This frothy deposit is a tell-tale sign that there are frog hoppers about. Treat them as you would aphids.*

fairly rare. Use a granular soil sterilant and wash the roots with an insecticide wash before replanting.

# Frog Hoppers

These are the green beetle-like creatures that exude a frothy deposit around young growing tips, commonly known as cuckoo spit. The pests will cause distortion and are best treated as for aphids.

# Mealy Bug

If a cotton wool-like mass is observed on the succulent *Pelargonium* stem it is likely to be mealy bug. Pick these off or dab with a cotton-bud soaked in methylated spirit.

# Red Spider Mite

These wingless mites are almost invisible to the eye, but the presence of small specks and webbing on the leaves and buds will herald their presence. Living in hot, dry conditions they will feed on the underneath of leaf surfaces. Fortunately, a collection of pelargoniums will not often be affected, but if other plants like fuchsia are grown in the same greenhouse, there could be a problem. Pelargoniums themselves do not attract many pests, but if grown among other plants then problems can escalate. Red spider mite is difficult to control because of its acquired resistance, but products are available. Damping down the floor space on a hot day will deter them.

# Sciarid Fly and Larva

Found in composts, especially peat-based types. They are tiny, whitish maggots which will turn into the small, black flies often seen hovering above the compost in a pot. The maggot will eat through the roots. Choose a product specifically for the purpose.

# Slugs and Snails

A common problem pair and known to all gardeners. Due to the high toxicity in slug killers and the dangers of wild animals such as hedge-hogs, toads and worms becoming affected by eating poisoned slugs and snails, many new preparations are now on the market. Some act on a birth control principle, some destroy by contact with the slug or snail and cause a shrinkage of the slime-forming organs. This type will remain active for six months. Old-fashioned ideas like beer-baits and grapefruit skins are also effective, but will have to be dealt with at regular intervals, which is not really much fun.

## Thrips

Thrips may be found in the greenhouse, but do not often attack pelargoniums. They leave a silvery, flecked appearance on leaves and flowers and are seen as small, blackish or light, golden flies. Treat with a systemic insecticide.

## Vine Weevil

The main damage is done by the larva which will chew into the base of the crown at the root, and the first indication of trouble will be the sudden death or wilting of a plant. On tipping out the pot you will see fat, white maggots with a brown head and usually in a curled posture. The beetle parent is black with a brown, hard body in a typical beetle form. The beetle will cut notches at the edges of foliage. Treat with a soil sterilising additive and use a soil-based compost, because vine weevils and their larvae seem to enjoy a peaty compost.

## Weeds

Weeds have to be classed as pests at all times but in a glasshouse they can grow at a very fast rate, soon reaching the flowering, then seedling stage. Seeds are dispersed into pots and on to the greenhouse bed where, apart from looking untidy, they can be hosts to insects such as green- and whitefly as well as providing hiding places for other problems like slugs, and so on. During the summer months when the door is left open, seeds can easily blow in, sometimes seeds may be present in poor quality compost and if the unthinkable is carried out, in other words the use of garden soil for greenhouse plants, then weed seeds will almost certainly soon germinate. It is simple just to pull up the seedlings as they germinate.

## Whitefly

Whitefly are the most common and most persistent of all pests in a greenhouse housing pelargoniums, especially the Regal types and some Scented and Species types. Again, this is a pest that is developing an immunity to modern pesticides. It is a tiny, moth-like insect capable of producing hundreds of eggs which hatch at variable speeds depending on the temperature. A warm day can suddenly produce a mist of white haze as a plant is moved, the young are able to reproduce at an early age and soon a massive infestation will be present if not controlled in good time. They also produce a honeydew deposit, which, after a while, will go black and, as well as looking unsightly, will impair the plant's growth due to the obstruction of light to the leaf through the black deposit. This should be washed away with a soap-based spray, at a solution of ¼tsp (1.25ml) to 2 pints of water (1.25 litres), which also washes away the fly's waxed coating, leaving it weakened and easier for insecticide to penetrate. Sap sucking, they leave wounds open to other diseases as well as transmitting disease themselves. The problem can be reduced by not growing other plants that are liked by whitefly in the same greenhouse, such as fuchsia, cucumber or tomato plants. Apart from systemic insecticides, only adults will be destroyed with normal whitefly killer. There are many on sale, some are more effective than others, and remember to change types now and again to prevent the immunity to certain insecticides. A programme of regular dosing at least weekly is necessary to continue the disposal of the infestation. A constant watch must be kept to ensure that the plants remain free of the fly and at the first signs of a reappearance the programme must begin again. If there are only one or two flies you can squash them on the leaves between finger and thumb. Much research has been done into the problems of whitefly, using predators as well as coloured, sticky sheets or cards. The use of predators is promising, but the main problems are that the most successful, which is a type of wasp, needs a supply of food at hand so that the whitefly is never totally destroyed, and the life cycle of the wasp sometimes is upset in our climate and the whole process discontinues.

## DISEASES

Diseases are in fact illnesses within the plant, as opposed to symptoms brought about by the presence of pests, although some disease problems can occur after a plant has been attacked by a pest, so to eradicate most pests will, in fact, prevent the plant from becoming sick. The *Pelargonium* is prone to fungal disease in the UK, due to the damp, dull, often cool, and still conditions, which are totally opposite to most of the natural environmental conditions it enjoys in the wild. Even though many cultivars have never seen their homeland, ancestral preference still reigns supreme in most types and varieties. To stimulate ideal requirements, good air circulation, winter warmth, a dry atmosphere and dry plant material and as much light and space as possible, will prevent many diseases taking hold. Constant inspection of the stock will highlight any problems before a massive problem is experienced.

## Blackleg

Blackleg is a condition found usually on newly-stuck cuttings and cuttings left to root, as well as newly potted, young plants. It will attack soft plant tissue and is seen at first as a black band at the base of the cutting at soil level. If not carefully removed, the fungus will spread up the stem as it is contagious. If the fungus is not too severe a cutting may be taken from the tip of the shoot. Be sure to sterilise the knife straight away and keep the cutting in quarantine for a while and remember that the taking of a cutting is only worthwhile if it is a very special plant that is affected and it is far safer to remove and destroy the whole cutting or plant. Giving the cuttings plenty of space between each one, making sure new, fresh compost is used, will help to keep blackleg confined. Prevention

is better than any cure with any pest or disease. Blackleg is a soil-borne fungus which affects Zonals more than other types of *Pelargonium*. Watering the cutting compost when the cuttings are stuck, when they have rooted and at the potting-up stage with a proprietary fungicide will help to prevent the problem, but there is no suitable cure.

## Botrytis (Grey Mould)

Poor drainage, poor ventilation, overcrowding, wet foliage and flowers will provide an ideal situation for these spores to develop. Petals which have fallen on benches or leaves as plant litter will soon show the signs of a grey, fluffy, mouldy patch which will become larger if

*Fig 80 An example of Botrytis (grey mould) and mildew.*

conditions suit. Make sure all dead and dying plant parts are removed and tidied away, disposing of any plant litter regularly. Young cuttings and seedlings are most prone, but any plant that has experienced damage could be affected. Cut away any diseased part, then dust with a fungicide. Do not use any affected piece as spores will be present. It is better to use a fungicide powder at this stage, because a spray could shoot the spores around as well as wet the foliage and flowers, giving a breeding ground for the fungal spores.

## Galls (Bacterial Fasciation)

Leaf or root gall is a type of plant cancer. Just at the soil level and at the stem it may be that gnarled, pale greenish-white growths are found, looking very much like small cauliflower curds. For the beginner, it is wise to destroy the plant completely. Modern peat-based compost seems to encourage this gall growth. There is no cure and it is thought that the complaint can be spread to other plants from water dropping on them and by contact. This is something to watch out for when buying plants, especially if they are potted into peat compost. All plants may be prone, but mainly Zonals and especially Miniatures and Dwarfs are affected.

## Mildew

Mildew may be found from time to time on the more shiny leaves, and sometimes on leaf stems, as small, greyish specks. Reduce watering and increase ventilation. Spray with a fungicide to kill the spores. This is not too much of a problem if treated.

## Rust (*Pelargonium* Rust)

This is the most serious of the diseases affecting the *Pelargonium*. Damp, dull, close conditions will encourage its presence. Rust is not observed in its early stages, unless the grower knows what to look for. Its first signs are on the underside of

the foliage on Zonals. Appearing first as small, rust-coloured, powdery specks, the spores will soon develop and begin to form a circle. When, in advanced stages, the circle joins, the centre of the affected part will fall away ready to begin its cycle again. The spores are water, soil and air borne and can be transferred from one plant to another by insects, birds and by human contact. Plants outside are affected during cool, damp summers. The nature of the situation will make it difficult to treat, but it is worth a try. Don't use the ground for pelargoniums next season, because in a mild winter the spores can survive.

In the greenhouse and conservatory, damp-ness, bad air circulation and lack of warmth will be a breeding ground for the spores. Fortun-ately it will mainly only attack plants with soft, lush leaves, so to keep plants growing hard and dry will be a deterrent. There is no cure. Prevention by good husbandry as well as a spray from time to time during acceptable conditions will help prevent the problem. If rust is found, immediately remove all affected foliage and place in a plastic bag and tie up the opening each time a leaf is removed to keep the spores from drifting. Destroy this totally. Do not take cuttings from the plant. Wash the hands and any apparatus used. Spray at weekly intervals with a fungicide for three or four weeks to weaken remaining spores. Warmth will dry out the atmosphere; also reduce watering as well as increase the air circulation whilst this prevention programme is carried out. Rust is widespread and present in some nurseries, so do check for it. Rust is present in most countries where pelargo-niums are grown in great numbers, and this is one reason why plants in the UK are inspected by Ministry officials.

## Stem Rot

Seedlings may suddenly develop a pinched stem and then fall over, and overcrowding or too thick a sowing will mean the problem can spread quickly. Use a watering of fungicide before sowing and at the pricking-out stage.

## Virus

There are many types and forms of virus, most of which will not be found in an amateur's collection. Some cause leaves or shoots to be twisted and distorted; some cause sporting, as well as a colour change and twisting and swelling. Any plant with these signs must be destroyed before the rest of the greenhouse is affected. Take care that any distortion is not just the result of sap-sucking insects such as green fly. Wilt and blight in many forms can affect pelargoniums; they are very serious, but rare in the amateur's stock. If strange growths are noticed it is wise to ask professional advice; take any suspect specimen in a sealed plastic bag, just in case!

## DISORDERS

Disorders are mainly due to a lapse in cultivation techniques or bad greenhouse management.

## Crook-neck and Proliferation (Hen and Chickens)

Crook-neck is found at the top of a flower-bearing stem (peduncle), just below the cluster of buds or blooms. The stem will be bent almost back on to itself and shaped like a crook, sometimes the stalk will crack and break, and disease may enter. Take off the flowering stem. It is caused usually at the beginning of the growing season, when extra water and feed is given. Reduce watering and feeding for a while. The Zonal range will be mainly affected. Crook-neck is a show fault, as is proliferation. 'Hen and chickens' is an old, common name for this occurrence in which a new flower head (umbel) rises out of the centre or side of a normally-placed flower head. This again is due to excessive watering and feeding at the beginning of the spring, when the plant has just begun to grow away after the winter's rest. Not only can it be a flower cluster, but sometimes a whole new growing plant is developed on a

sometimes leafy shoots occur on the flower-head

*Fig 81 Proliferation – 'Hen and Chickens'.*

103

*Fig 82 Crook-neck.*

long stem. This must be removed before it saps the plant's energy.

## *Oedema* (Dropsy)

*Oedema* is found almost exclusively on Ivy-leaved types and varieties, and is often mistaken for *Pelargonium* rust. Small, shallow, corky blisters appear on the underside of the foliage and, as they turn light brown and scab over, they can be seen on the upper surface. Bad or inexperienced cultivation is the cause. When Ivy-leaved varieties have been left to dry out, or water has been reduced so that the plant can cope with the colder months better, the outer tissue or skin of the leaf becomes hard and strong. The plant has perhaps been cut back and when copious watering is commenced, the plant cannot take up so much so

quickly at one time, so the cells burst. This leaves the scars that you will see. Take off the damaged leaves, reduce watering and feeding for a week or two and improve air circulation to assist in the drying-out process and the plant will soon right itself and grow new leaves. Dropsy usually only occurs once in this early season.

## Reddening of Foliage

This disorder can be caused by opposite conditions, in the greenhouse. Sudden spring sunshine through the glass may be too much for a plant that has been housed in a dull situation and the older foliage will turn a russet-red colour which is actually quite attractive. These leaves will not turn green again, and must be removed so that the plant may use energy to concentrate on new growth which will adjust as it grows to the brighter conditions. Draughts or very cold spells at the beginning of summer will also cause the leaves to change colour in the garden, as well as the greenhouse. Leaves may turn yellow in cold, draughty conditions. Zonals are normally prone to this foliage discolouration, but Regals are also known to suffer when sometimes just the outer edges to the leaves will turn red. Take off the leaves particularly from plants growing outside in beds, because the leaves will in time fall off and can go undetected in a bedding situation, so causing fungal problems. Maybe a deficiency or imbalance in the compost is to blame. It is best to stop feeding for a while and note the condition of the new growth. If the growth is improved, feeding can begin again, using a quarter strength, liquid general feed and stepping up gradually to the normal rate.

In conclusion, if any treatment is required, weigh up the pros and cons between chemical and organic or natural products. Even if the latter are not quite as effective, give Nature a chance and only then switch to man-made sources.

CHAPTER 12

# The Pelargonium Grower's Calendar

The following chronological guide is intended only for general advice, in a sequence that should be of particular assistance to beginners. Bear in mind that months may not always be average as some seasons may overlap by as much as four weeks especially during very mild winters in the UK – however, the seasonal pattern will usually return and become stable during the summer period. Even so, there is a marginal variability between the north and south of the UK, or between cooler areas such as coastlines or frost pockets and more sheltered places and this should be taken into account. (Note that the month in brackets in the headings below refers to the appropriate month in the Southern hemisphere.)

## JANUARY (JULY)

At this time of year watering should be undertaken very carefully – if in doubt, don't water. Water used during the colder months should be warm. Ventilation should be checked, and on sunny afternoons, unless the weather is freezing, leave the door open for an hour during the early afternoon, as this will be beneficial. Check that the glass is clean as winter dirt soon builds up both inside and out. Wash off the outside with warm water incorporating a squirt of washing-up liquid. On the inside glass wipe down only, then dry it over, because moisture levels have to be kept low in the atmosphere during these longer, dark days. If

thermal curtains or plastic double glazing is used, wipe this over too and remove any sagging, so that water or condensation will not settle.

Continue the picking-over programme. During the winter it is even more important that stem tissue is not damaged, so when removing leaves, gently press the leaf stalk (petiole) upwards from underneath towards the stem. A

*Fig 83 Bloom of 'Blue Beard', a fairly new Ivy-leaved variety.*

slight crack will be heard and with a gentle pull the leaf should fall away having separated from its stem at a natural point, leaving only a small wound without any torn tissue. If the dead or dying leaf cannot be removed in this way, it will be safer to cut half-way down the petiole, leaving the remaining piece on the plant to dry and fall away naturally. When this happens remove the piece as well as any fallen blooms, stipules or leaves. Sometimes there will be a wound, perhaps after some dying part has had to be removed with a clean sharp knife, and in these colder spells it would be a precaution to dust the wound with a fungicide powder.

Check that heaters and thermostats are working properly, as this is the time of year when really frosty weather can strike suddenly. If very severe, freezing weather is forecast and the greenhouse is kept only just warm enough, the heater may not be able to cope with a sudden plummeting of temperatures, so turn up the heat or adjust the thermostat, to be on the safe side. Near the glass, plants can be covered with newspaper as a temporary measure, this should be removed during the day except on very frosty days. If the newspaper is loosely scrunched up into a sausage shape and placed between plants and glass, a fair amount of protection will be obtained, but take away and renew any paper that becomes soaked from the dampness of the glass.

With care, rake over the surface of pots that have become caked with moss or algae. Although this should not be the case, mossy growth does sometimes occur, especially with plants in the cooler, darker part of the greenhouse.

You can now sow the first batch of F1 hybrids in the propagator to ensure a flowering display from about early June.

## FEBRUARY (AUGUST)

Continue to water only when necessary at the beginning of the month, perhaps increasing towards the end of February, especially if some warm days have arrived. Do not wet foliage. Some of the tuberous *Pelargonium* species will enjoy a delicate watering now and foliage could be showing. If the propagator is in use, the cutting of such tubers can be done, and left to chit in a light place. Cuttings taken off plants brought in from the garden last autumn, should be well rooted and can be potted up. Seedlings can be pricked out and watered carefully with an anti-fungus solution. Sow F2 hybrids in heat.

Keep the atmosphere buoyant and leave the door open when the weather permits. Plants for summer shows should receive their last but one stop (depending on the date of the chosen shows), but continue to dis-bud. The last of the show schedules should be to hand now, so plan carefully which ones to support. Continue picking-over, as sudden spring sunshine through the glass can cause the leaves to discolour. If the sun is strong protect vulnerable plants and newly potted cuttings as well as pricked seedlings until they become stronger.

Order new plants from specialist nurseries now, if you have not already done so, or your preferences may be sold out. Some firms sell ready chitted seed and young seedlings and the end of this month, if the greenhouse is heated, will be an ideal time to get some, so that they will bloom well early in the summer.

## MARCH (SEPTEMBER)

Spring is now nearly here, but do not be too hasty, there may well be more frost and adverse weather conditions. Picking-over, careful watering and increased ventilation, as well as more seedlings to prick out and the early ones to pot on, will supply plenty of work this month. It is wise to keep up with all tasks before the spring really arrives. Sow self-gathered seeds this month, these may be species or some results from crossings and don't forget to keep records of any breeding results up to date.

A liquid feed should be increased for all plants potted two months previously and earlier, as there is only about six weeks' supply of fertiliser in a soil-based compost and less than that in most peat-based ones. During the growing season, feeding should commence five to six weeks after potting.

Cuttings intended to be trained as standards or shapes should be taken at the beginning of the month and, if conditions are good, they can be taken in February, however, the stock plant is often not fit at that time. Supply heat at the base of the pot or tray. Keep these cuttings, once rooted, growing at all times as evenly as possible by over-potting slightly. Cuttings for trained specimens should be ready to flower in fourteen to eighteen months' time, depending on variety. They should not be allowed to flower until the head is well formed.

Show plants should have their last stop in the middle of the month. Check for any insect pests, that have over-wintered, they will be evident on warmer days and will begin to breed, so take action. Slugs could be a problem in the greenhouse beds during the winter.

# APRIL (OCTOBER)

Regals could be in bud now, so increase the feed of a high potash type to encourage giant-sized blooms that will be so welcome at this time of the year as houseplants. Start taking cuttings of over-wintered plants. Continue tidying, potting and watering the plants and increase the feed to half strength of a general formula at each watering. Change or rotate special need feeds as necessary, however, a high potash feed will encourage future flowering. On warm but not very sunny days, a light spray of a foliar feed early in the day will be beneficial. A spray of magnesium or Epsom Salts will make the foliage strong and give it a rich, green appearance. The recommended dosage is 1 tablespoon into 2 gallons of water (25 ml to 10 litres) and because Epsom Salts is a crystal it will need to be mixed with hot water to speed up and ensure that it dissolves.

Do the final pinch to plants for the greenhouse, conservatory, patio pots and garden bedding. Cuttings may be taken from these pinchings if they are suitable or required. Remember that greenhouse space will be becoming short, plants will continue to grow and their rate of growth to increase greatly soon, so keep space available to allow the plants plenty of room. Daylight hours will increase markedly during this month, enabling work to be carried out during the evening, even if there is no artificial light in the greenhouse.

On mild days, plants intended for outdoor use can begin their hardening off programme; a cold frame will be a help, but to place the plants outside for even a short time will also be beneficial to them. A light shower of rain will be enjoyed too, but make sure it does not occur in late afternoon, because the plants will still be wet at night. Warm sun during late spring can raise the temperature in a glasshouse far too high, so watch out for this. The door may be left open all day on good days, but remember to close it at night and to bring in plants from outside airings before the chill night air appears. This early sun could cause a disorder or two, so learn to recognise this if it happens. Ensure that automatic windows and louvres are free and in working order. Think about summer shading during this month. Plants ordered for spring delivery may now have arrived. Remember to acclimatise the batch and shade from sun and bright light for a day or two.

Plant up hanging baskets and leave them in the greenhouse. If they are hung up by the glass, protect them in hot sun. Patio pots and window-boxes can be planted up now and left in the greenhouse too. Begin their hardening off programme a week after planting up. Now it can be seen how many and what sort of plants are available for bedding schemes, so draw up the bedding display plan. April is one of the busiest months in the garden generally, so try

Fig 84 'Pink Bonanza' is a very attractive Regal Pelargonium which blooms early in the season.

not to neglect any aspect of cultivation while catching up on your other horticultural tasks.

## MAY (NOVEMBER)

May marks the start of the *Pelargonium* season proper. In the greenhouse and conservatory and on indoor window-sills, all types of *Pelargonium* will either be in flower or in bud. Foliage will be of a mature size and of good colour; however, the ornamental varieties will still not have their true, splendid shades until they can spend more time out of doors, in the not-too-strong sunshine. Cuttings should have rooted and those taken now will root readily and still give weeks of blooms later in the summer. Seedlings of F1 and F2 varieties are now into their penultimate pot sizes before being used as bedding plants. Species seedlings

and your own hybrids will have developed the first two sets of leaves and perhaps a further pair. Pot them on at regular intervals. Water more often, in warm periods, for mature plants this could be daily. Feed can also be increased. Make sure that greenhouse windows are opened in the mornings, and leave the door ajar (if necessary make a wire doorway to stop animals entering). Shading will almost certainly be required from now on.

Continue picking over and turning plants. In the middle of the month all plants destined for outdoors should be day-hardened. Unless night-time frosts are forecast, the plants should be left outside in a sheltered position towards the end of the month. Beware of late frosts which will wreak havoc with young, soft growth. If possible, plant up patio pots and tubs and leave them in the glasshouse (if there is room this job can be done in April). Tubs and pots should be hardened off in the same way as individual plants. The completion of the hardening off should be in the last weekend of May, after which most frosts will have hopefully passed by. All patio planters, window-boxes and hanging baskets can now be sited in their summer position.

Prepare the beds for bedding and water them if it does not rain, consult your planting plan, then bed out. Plants for pot and show work will be growing well, do not remove any more buds after the middle of the month unless the plant appears overcrowded. Treat any pest or disease, or take preventive action. Early blooming Regals, especially those that have been used as an indoor display, will have finished flowering now, so neaten the plants and feed and if possible stand them in a sheltered outside situation to ripen the new growth and allow them to recover before taking cuttings. Cuttings will not need heat now.

## JUNE (DECEMBER)

This is the month of panic for exhibitors. Have schedules been read thoroughly and entries been returned by the last date? Is the area and hall familiar to you? Is your transport reliable? Are the plants in tiptop condition? The last few days before a show should be spent on finer details – tidy up the plants, stake them ready for transporting, write out a clean label, wash the pots and have a good night's sleep the night before.

Don't neglect the rest of your collection during this period. June is often very warm in the UK, too warm for a greenhouse to be closed all day with no shading put up. It may be that the floor will have to be wetted in the morning to help keep down the afternoon temperature. Some blooms will be going over and it is worth removing these before they begin to fall or go rotten through water lying in the head. Plants outside can be fed now. All pelargoniums may be housed out of doors and

this will reduce your work as well as give the plants a holiday. Watch out for pests. Visit some shows and specialist nurseries, as they will be a blaze of colour this month. Order next year's catalogue, and make a note of the plants seen at shows and nurseries that you could grow next year.

## JULY (JANUARY)

There will still be some shows to enjoy this month, perhaps while you are on holiday. You can always visit nurseries while away on holiday too. Before going on your annual break, pay attention to the needs of the plants, especially their needs for the long term, including the removal of the blooms and buds which will open while the holiday is in progress. Try to encourage a neighbour to take an interest and repay the favour while the neighbour is away, this way plants will not be neglected during holiday absences.

July is the best month for taking cuttings of temperamental pelargoniums, such as some Angel varieties and some Species. Seeds should be forming on plants and if they are to be kept, gather them while dry and store in a waxed envelope, clearly marked with the name, date, parentage, and so on. Take off all fading blooms if the seed is not wanted, this will ensure following blooms and will not sap the plant's energy. Watering will be frequently required and feeding should be continued. Cuttings for the provision of next year's show plants must be taken by the end of the month, to give the plant a good headstart. Some specimens may need repotting and earlier cuttings will need potting up. Mark plants that have not come up to your expectations and find out whether it is just the cultivation; if so take steps to rectify it. They may just not be suitable for the type of situation required, and if not, give them away to make room for different varieties to be tried and tested. A further spray of Epsom Salts will be beneficial.

Fig 85 A pelargonium seed ready for dispersal.

## AUGUST (FEBRUARY)

Regal cuttings take well this month. Other types can be also taken. If holidays are to be taken this month, don't forget to leave the plants in good hands. Tubs, patio pots and troughs may require a topping up of fresh compost, especially if rain and wind has compacted the top. Take a few cuttings from the non-flowering shoots of these plants. Show plants will require a rest period, so take off all the flowers and unwanted growth. Plants grown as indoor specimens will repay the efforts of a period outside to enjoy the fresh atmosphere and gentle rains. Leaves can become very dusty indoors without an occasional spray. Hanging baskets might need a revamp, and if plants are looking sad, replace them with younger ones, water them in well and do not forget to feed hanging baskets all summer. Seed gathering continues. Pot on the plants recently purchased.

## SEPTEMBER (MARCH)

You can safely remove the shading now, because temperatures and sun power are dropping daily and the plants should be mature enough to cope with the odd sunshine spell. Water will not be required as much as in the growing months, nor feeding, but still use half strength at each water. At the end of the month, plans must be in operation to make room and the facilities to bring in plants from outside. Pot up any rooted cuttings. Close the doors at night. Begin to cut back any plants from outside beds you intend to keep, and dust them with a fungicide powder. Check very carefully for pests and diseases, and remove all dead and yellowing foliage. Patio pots would be happy left planted up if there is room in the greenhouse or conservatory, where their colour may still be enjoyed. If they have to be stored in smaller pots, take some cuttings and cut the blooms for the house as they will last a long time in water. Inspect the glasshouse for maintenance requirements, which should be done before the plants are brought in for the winter, when space will make jobs easier. Any wood preserving or painting should be carried out on clean, dry, dust-free surfaces with non-toxic materials. Look on the container to check its suitability where plants are concerned. And finally clean the glass inside and out.

## OCTOBER (APRIL)

Continue to pot up the following year's show stock. Heaters should be checked over and cleaned at the beginning of the month and brought into action. Use an air circulating fan now as well as in the summer. The greenhouse which will be housing pelargoniums must be frost-free. A temperature of 5–6°C (40–42°F) will keep plants ticking over until the spring. Raise the temperature and some plants will be encouraged to bloom through the winter, watering will need to be kept to a minimum, but more will be required in higher temperatures. On fine, mild days have the doors and windows open. If you plan to use a thermal curtain to conserve heat in one area of the glasshouse or to use total double glazing-style polythene sheeting, this should be erected at the end of the month. Make sure that windows are clean before the sheeting is put up because as much light as possible must be admitted. Send for catalogues from nurseries and seedsmen. Try not to overcrowd the greenhouse or conservatory and take a few plants indoors to spend the winter on a well lit but cool windowsill. Miniatures will bloom readily during the winter in a warm room with plenty of light.

## NOVEMBER (MAY)

Keep the glass clean and the heaters in good condition and have a reserve supply of heating material. Continue to pick over the plants. On good days give them extra air by opening the doors and windows, however you must close these during mid-afternoon, before the temperature outside begins to drop. Keep a special eye on the hygiene of the greenhouse during this month. Next year's show plants should be nearly ready for their final pots now. Show schedules are usually available, so write off to those shows you are planning to visit or exhibit at. If a plant was entered at a show last year, the chances are that automatic mailing will follow. Glance through the new season's catalogues so that you can choose and order your requirements. It is a good plan to request delivery at a time when the new plants can be accommodated and worked on and, as it is no use plants arriving when you are on holiday, you should stipulate an approximate delivery date.

## DECEMBER (JUNE)

This is the month in which you can take it easy to some degree. Reflect on the previous season, plan to rectify all problems and improve on even the best of your previous achievements. Purchase seed at the beginning of the month and sow the F1s in order to have blooms in June. The propagator will be needed for early sowings. There will still be picking over and some general checking to do on the plants.

If you are thinking of becoming generally more active in the hobby, there are many local and some national societies who would welcome newcomers. A subscription to one of these societies would be a long-lasting Christmas gift, as would be a gift voucher to be spent at a specialist nursery or garden centre.

# Appendices

## I PLANT LISTS

### Scented-Leaved Pelargonium

Many of the species have scented leaves, as well as some plants that have been hybridised and known for many years. The correct title is 'Aromatic-leaved', but this is not at all a popular description, so although 'scented' usually refers to flowers, Scented-leaved is the generally accepted name. These plants can conveniently be placed in further groups, depending on the individual aroma or scent of the foliage, and are Fruit, Flower, Spice and Herb, Aromatic or Pungent.

In the list below, each type of aroma or scent is noted and then a selection of the plants of that scent are listed and described, together with their parental origins (where known).

### Fruit

These scents include orange, lemon, strawberry, filbert nut, lime, citron, apple, coconut, peach, cedar and balsam.

**'Prince of Orange'** A *P.crispum* hybrid. Orange-scented, a tallish but compact plant with glossy medium-sized foliage of fresh green. The flowers are large for the type and mauve.

**'Lemon Fancy'** A *P.scabrum* hybrid. Lemon-scented. Rough, triangular, medium-sized leaves. The flowers are medium-sized and mauve. It needs pinching out to prevent it becoming straggly.

**'Concolor Lace'** A cross of *P.capitatum x P.fulgidum* Filbert nut-scented. A small plant, useful for hanging pot culture. The foliage is light green to greyish and deeply cut. It has many small scarlet blooms.

**P.odoratissimum,** a true species Apple-scented. A small, hummock-shaped plant with kidney-shaped leaves, and small whitish flowers. Sometimes the flowering stems become long. This extremely versatile plant is suitable for basket work as well as in the kitchen and in pot-pourri.

**Nervosum, P.x nervosum** Lime-scented. A neat plant of medium height with mid-green shiny leaves, and mauve flowers.

### Flower

Rose, balsam, rose/mint, lavender, cedar and pine.

**'Attar of Roses'** Rose-scented. Delicate rose fragrance from the grey-green leaves. It does not grow too tall. The flowers are small, pink to mauve. A very popular variety, with many uses.

**P.capitatum** This plant is rose-scented, sometimes with a citrus tone when the plants are in bloom. The main species is grown as a crop to extract oil for the perfumery industry. The mauve to pink flowers are held in a cluster, the seed heads are large and the leaves ruffled and velvety in the form of shallow lobes with toothed edges.

**P.graveolens** Rose-citrus-scented. Heavily scented, green grey lobed and cut leaves. The blooms are rosy-pink with purple marks on top petals.

**'Lady Plymouth'** *P.graveolens variegata* Rose-mint scent. A variegated plant with lobed and well-cut cream and green leaves. Lovely as a house plant. There is a grey-leaved form, called 'Grey Lady Plymouth'. The blooms are small and pink to mauve.

**'Rober's Lemon Rose'** *P.graveolens x tomentosum* Rose-mint-scented. A charming plant which will grow to 2ft (60cm). The felty, triangular and lobed leaves are deeply cut and the flowers are deep pink with purple veining.

**'Variegated Fragrans'** *P. x fragrans variegata* Pine-herb-scented. The foliage is small and cream with light green. The flowers are tiny, white with mauve markings.

**'Clorinda'** One of the Uniques with a strongly-scented foliage. Cedar-scented. The large leaves are lobed and the blooms are large and bright pink with purple marks. This is a shrubby plant. There is also a golden variegated form.

## Spice and Herb

Southernwood, peppermint, menthol, nutmeg, ginger.

**P.abrotanifolium** A lovely species. Southernwood-scented. The foliage is tiny, feathery and grey-green. It is not a tall grower and is useful for flower arranging. The flowers may be deep pink or white.

**P.tomentosum** A species with Peppermint-scented leaves. The lovely, soft flannel-like leaves are quite large. The plant can become large and scrambling. It has whitish blooms. There is also a form crossed with *P.quercifolium*

which gives *P.tomentosum* a brown blotch in the centre of the foliage. This form is called 'Chocolate Peppermint'.

**P. x fragrans** Nutmeg or Eucalyptus-scented. A small plant overall. The flowers are white with mauve markings. A popular variety and very useful in the kitchen and in pot-pourri.

**'Torento'** Ginger-scented. Kidney-shaped to round, shiny leaves. The flowers are medium-sized and rose-lavender coloured. A neat plant.

## Aromatic or Pungent

These aromas cannot be defined clearly and some people do not find them pleasant, but like all the scented range, it does depend on an individual's sense of smell. The plants in this range seem to have sticky leaves, so are not suitable for use in pot-pourri.

**P.denticulatum** A true species with very finely divided foliage which is sticky to the touch. Attractive for flower arranging uses. The flowers are small and deep mauve-pink.

**P.quercifolium** Known widely as 'the Oak-leaf Pelargonium'. Its leaves are shaped like those of an oak, and have a dark blotch in the centre of the dark green foliage. The blooms are lovely, being large and mauve with dark markings in the upper petals. In some forms the petals are serrated.

# Unique Pelargonium

**'Claret Rock Unique'** Claret-rose blooms with red shading. A strong grower, the leaves are dark green.

**'Paton's Unique'** It has neon-rose, largish flowers with maroon veining and is very pretty.

**'Pretty Polly'** A small growing plant with frilled flowers of shaded pink and salmon.

*Fig 86 A pretty Unique variety, 'Paton's Unique'.*

**'Rollinson's Unique'** This is a tall plant which is a little straggly with mid-green leaves. The blooms are a beautiful rich magenta-purple.

**'Scarlet Unique'** This plant has medium-sized flowers of scarlet.

**'White Unique'** This Unique has large blooms of white with some purple veining, and it is a tall growing and leafy plant.

There are a few Unique types that are known as 'Hybrid Uniques', which were raised in America. They are more compact in stature than the type.

**'Bolero'** This plant has purple-rose flowers on a large-leaved plant.

**'Carefree'** It has delicate red blooms with a white throat.

**'Polka'** This plant has a slightly variegated foliage and orange-red flowers.

## Regal Pelargonium

The plant lists in this book contain only a handful of all the varieties available and, because the main cultivar lists are vast and could fill many books, it must be realised that only a few can be discussed here. The best way to collect lists of most cultivars available for sale, is to apply to specialist nurseries whose addresses will be found in the gardening press, or in the magazines of specialist societies. Please do not forget that these catalogues are expensive to produce, so the nursery will have to make a minimal charge to cover costs and postage.

**'Aztec'** Perhaps one of the best-known Regals. The blooms have a white base and deep brownish-red markings. A compact plant. A fringed-petalled form has recently been introduced called 'Fringed Aztec'.

**'Amethyst'** A deep lavender plant, which gets darker on account of shading on the upper petals, together with maroon feathering. There is a light mark in the centre of each petal which is almost white.

**'Carisbrooke'** This plant has carmine-blotched rose-pink petals.

**'Grand Slam'** Another popular Regal, together with its sport 'Lavender Grand Slam'.

Fig 87 'Fringed Aztec' is a variant of a well-known Regal variety.

It also has other sports worth looking for. It has large rose-red flowers whose upper petals are marked with purple-red.

**'Harbour Lights'** A new variety with frilled blooms, that has salmon-red upper petals and lower petals in a lighter shade with dark feathering.

**'La Paloma'** This plant has beautiful large, white blooms, with the palest mauve flush on the top petals.

**'Love Song'** A variegated foliage variety. The leaves are an unusual shape and are very deeply serrated. The blooms are pink and maroon. A new variety which is bushy.

**'Morwenna'** This Regal has almost black flowers which are very large. It is a compact and vigorous plant.

**'Spot-on-Bonanza'** A sport from 'Bonanza'. It has pink spots and speckling on a near white ground.

**'South American Bronze'** A tall growing, usually straggly plant which has bronze blooms with a pencil edge of white.

**'Violetta'** A compact plant with silvery, violet flowers.

**'Wellington'** This plant has large orange flowers lightening to pink at the throat, while the top petals are marked in a plum shade.

**'Wookey'** A plant which has cherry-red blooms and salmon flushing. The upper petals are marked in maroon or near black.

## Angel Pelargonium, Miniature and Dwarf Regal

**'Beromunster'** Dwarf Regal that is pale pink, with cerise blotching on all petals.

**'Captain Starlight'** A plant which has large, round soft mauve flowers with darker top petals and maroon blotching. An Angel variety.

**'Catford Belle'**   This is a compact plant with many smallish mauve blooms with purple markings, the petals sometimes have a slight frilled look. An Angel variety introduced by Mr Arthur Langley Smith.

**'Hemingstone'**   An Angel which has large lavender flowers with dark blotching on the upper petals.

**'Little Love'**   A miniature Regal which can be difficult to propagate. The small, soft, serrated leaves are tightly packed on an upright plant. The flowers are soft mauve with some markings.

**'Rita Scheen'**   A variegated-leaved Angel. It has small pale mauve flowers with maroon markings.

**'Tip Top Duet'**   This Angel has mauve as the base colour with very dark maroon top petals.

**'Velvet Duet'**   An Angel which has darkest plum on all petals, with a little paler blushing towards the outer edges.

## Zonal Pelargonium

The Basic Zonals will be listed first, and they will be divided into two sections depending on their flower formation.

### Single-flowered Varieties

**'Ainsdale Sixty'**   A new variety with deep pink petals and white 'eye' to the two upper petals. It has a well-zoned foliage.

*Fig 88 'Tip Top Duet'. An Angel with strong colouration bred by the author.*

**'Ashfield Serenade'** Large, lavender-pink flowers on a stocky plant.

**'Dryden'** 'Geranium Lake' with a large, white eye.

**'Edward Humphris'** For a good white, this variety is an old favourite.

**'Highfields Choice'** A good variety for showing purposes. It is pink with a lavender hue and has dark green foliage with a zone.

**'Mr Wren'** Another variety that has been around for years. It has a white base to its petals, but with striking vermilion 'brush-strokes'. It can be a tall and straggly plant, but worthwhile to have in any collection.

**'Sundridge Surprise'** This plant has large purple blooms with a white eye and a dark zone on mid-green leaf.

**'Vera Dillon'** It has magenta petals with a scarlet-orange base colour.

## Semi-double and Double Flowered Varieties

**'Blues'** A newly introduced semi-double. It is white-eyed and shocking pink with a stocky habit.

**'Creamery'** Near yellow double which is more a deep cream when grown well. It can be hard to grow, but one to have in a collection.

**'Bold Sunrise'** A fairly new introduction which has semi-double blooms of deep salmon.

**'Duke of Devonshire'** A double form which has deep pink and light red petals with a white eye.

**'E.Dabner'** A double that has crimson suffused with white blooms.

*Fig 89 'Creamery', the nearest to a yellow colouration to date.*

**'Garibaldi'** A pretty-coloured double bloom which has white overlaid by a soft salmon.

**'Hermione'** An old, pure white double.

**'Highfields Prima Donna'** A good exhibition double. The flowers are rose-pink.

**'Orange Fizz'** It may be difficult to grow as all the orange-coloured Zonals tend to be. It is a bushy plant with double orange flowers.

**'Pac Rospen'** Quite a modern variety with soft purple petals, marked with red spots on the upper ones. Compact grower.

**'Pretty Petticoat'** A full double with white petals, heavily marked on the margin with soft pink.

**'Something Special'** Another good show variety. A double which is Empire rose with darker shading towards the centre of the bloom.

**'Wedding Royale'** This compact plant could almost be listed with the 'Rosebud' section, as it has double ruffled carmine-rose blooms. The leaves are medium green with a dark zone. It is a compact plant.

**'William Tell'** A double with many names ranging from 'Old King Cole', 'Frogmore', 'Royal Purple', to 'Brooke's Purple'. It is a lovely Tyrian purple colour with a darker edging to the petals.

## Irene Varieties

**'Dark Red Irene'** The darkest red.

**'Electra'** Bluish soft red.

**'Glacier Queen'** White.

**'Irene'** The original variety with medium red blooms.

**'Party Dress'** Pretty baby-pink.

**'Springtime Irene'** Pale salmon.

## Fiat Varieties

**'Enchantress Fiat'** Soft salmon-pink.

**'Fiat'** Soft orange-pink.

**'Fiat Princess'** Palest salmon. Serrated edges to the petals.

**'Fiat Queen'** This Fiat has serrated coral petals.

**'Royal Fiat'** Pretty serrated shrimp pink petals which fade to whitish-coral at the edge.

## 'Deacon' Varieties

**'Deacon Arlon'** The only white 'Deacon'. The buds are a pale green-cream before opening, and this white does not turn pink in the sun.

**'Deacon Birthday'** Salmon and peach in shades.

**'Deacon Bonanza'** Pretty magenta-pink.

**'Deacon Fireball'** Vibrant scarlet.

**'Deacon Jubilant'** Cerise with a well-zoned foliage.

**'Deacon Peacock'** Not the best of the 'Deacons', but it has a pale butterfly variegation in the foliage. Blooms are orange to scarlet.

**'Deacon Picotee'** White petals with a roseate shading.

**'Deacon Sunburst'** This plant is a delicate orange.

## 'Bird's Egg' Varieties

**'Double Bird's Egg'** Plum spotting on light magenta petals.

**'Plenty'** Double flowers which are off-white with rose-pink spots.

**'Purple Bird's Egg'** It is deep mauve to purple, making the darker spotting on the single blooms rather difficult to see.

**'White Bird's Egg'** White single blooms with rose spotting.

## Cactus-flowered Varieties

**'Attraction'** A lovely single form which is camellia-rose with coral stripings.

**'Fire Dragon'**    Double signal-red blooms.

**'Mrs Salter Bevis'**    This plant is more dwarf in habit with very pretty lavender-pink double flowers.

**'Noel'**    A double, white.

**'Spitfire'**    A variety with bi-coloured foliage which is a bit difficult to grow. It is single with bright red flowers.

## Rosebud Varieties

**'Apple Blossom Rosebud'**    This is the best known of the type and is freely available from good garden centres, in early summer. The tight white buds are of a greenish tone, opening to white petals edged with rose-pink.

**'Pink Rambler'**    Its blooms are pink and darker on the reverse.

**'Purple Rambler'**    Dark magenta to light purple.

**'Rosebud Supreme'**    Blood red.

**'Rococo'**    A new variety. Very large pink flowers and unusual foliage.

**'Wedding Royale'**    See list, Basic Zonal on page 118.

## Stellar Varieties

**'Stellar Arctic Star'**    A large, white single.

**'Stellar Cathay'**    A salmon single.

**'Stellar Grenadier'**    A fiery scarlet double flower.

**'Stellar Hanaford Star'**    A pretty single with deep salmon blooms.

*Fig 90 'Grenadier', a double-flowered Stellar-type Zonal.*

**'Stellar Snowflake'**  A double with white flowers. Take care that the blooms do not go pink in full sun.

## Fingered Varieties

**'Formosum'**  A large plant, with deeply-lobed leaves. The blooms are semi-double and are salmon with white tips to petals.

**'Playmate'**  It is miniature to dwarf in habit. The flowers are semi-double to double and salmon coloured.

**'Urchin'**  A scarlet dwarf to miniature.

## Tulip-flowered Varieties

**'Patricia Andrea'**  Salmon.

**'Pink Pandora'**  Pink blooms.

**'Red Pandora'**  Soft red flowers.

## Miscellaneous Types

**'Distinction'**  This plant has medium-green leaves with a narrow, pencilled zone. The flowers are of primitive form and currant-red.

**'Floral Cascade'**  A *frutetorum* type with double rose-coral blooms. The foliage is dark green, small and with a central blotch of brown.

**'Honeywood Suzanne'**  A *frutetorum* type. A dwarf with a compact habit. It has delicate, double blooms of white to palest pink with darker flushing.

**'Jeanne'**  It has single flowers of salmon-serrated petals. They are sometimes known as 'Carnation-flowered' types.

**'Mauretania'**  A 'Phlox' type having off-white blooms and a coral 'halo' at the centre of the single flower.

**'Phlox New Life'**  A single which is white with a salmon-pink eye.

**'Single New Life'**  This one has single blooms with a white ground which is irregularly striped with bright vermilion, or petals of either white or vermilion. It is thought to be a sport from Vesuvius. One for the collector.

**'Skelly's Pride'**  This is another 'Carnation' type with single salmon petals that are serrated at the edge.

**'The Prostrate Boar'**  A *frutetorum* type. It is lovely for an unusual hanging basket plant. The thin, trailing stems have small, dark green leaves blotched heavily in brown. Flowers are single, coral and of a primitive form held on long flower stalks.

**'Wirral Cascade'**  Double red flowers on a *frutetorum* type plant.

## Ornamental-foliaged Varieties

**'Caroline Schmidt'**  A popular bi-colour which has red double flowers. Good for outside work.

**'Contrast'**  A tri-colour with single scarlet flowers.

**'Dovedale'**  A golden-leaved variety. This is a new introduction with semi-double white blooms which is unusual.

**'Flower of Spring'**  An old variety, good for bedding. It has single, scarlet flowers, and is a bi-colour.

**'Golden Ears'**  A bronze-leaved Stellar with a golden-leaved margin. The blooms are typical 'Stellar' shape and are orange-red.

**'Golden Gates'**  This plant has golden foliage and single salmon-orange blooms.

*Fig 91 'Single New Life' is an unusual Zonal with many variations in both petal colour and markings.*

**'Mont Blanc'**   A bi-colour with white, single flowers.

**'Mr (Mrs) Henry Cox'**   Another old favourite, 'Henry Cox' is used in bedding or as a pot plant. It has tri-coloured foliage and is very brilliant outdoors in a good summer. The blooms of this plant are single, coral.

**'Pink Happy Thought'**   A butterfly-marked type. The flowers are single and fuchsia-pink. There is a red-flowered form called 'A Happy Thought'.

**'Rene Roue'**   This ornamental-foliaged plant is a double with red flowers and is a compact growing bi-colour.

**'Skies of Italy'**   A golden tri-colour with double soft orange blooms.

**'Sophie Dumeresque'**   This plant is a single with mandarin orange flowers. It is a tri-colour with attractive gold-cream leaves and a bright zone.

**'Sundridge Moonlight'**   It is golden-leaved with no zone and has single blooms of pure white.

**'Susie 'Q''**   A good show variety with gold leaves and single soft-pink blooms.

**'Tapestry'**   This plant has single flowers which are salmon. It is a tri-colour that needs a little extra care and attention.

**'The Czar'** An old cultivar. It has a bronze zone and light green, nearly gold, leaves. The flowers are single and vermilion.

**'Turkish Delight'** It has an unusual leaf colouration of golden central pattern and reddish-bronze zone with bright green outer margin. The blooms are single with orange-scarlet flowers.

## FI Hybrids

**'Breakaway'** A series of self-branching and early-flowering varieties of red, salmon and pink colours.

**'Diamond'** The colour range of this variety is cherry, rose, and scarlet, and it is a free-flowering and fairly compact plant with deep zoning.

**'Orbit'** It is compact and early flowering, in a range of many colours including white.

**'Pulsar'** This is a range of good growing plants in pink, red, rose, salmon, white and bi-colour.

**'Ringo'** The usual colours on well-zoned foliage.

**'Summer Showers'** The FI Ivy-leaf. It has many attractive colours including a lovely magenta.

## F2 Hybrids or Open-pollinated Varieties

**'Firebird'** An intense scarlet bloom with medium-zoned leaves.

**'Imp'** This is a fairly new variety bred from FIs.

**'Sprite'** This variety has mixed colours and depths of zone and is a dwarf plant.

Fig 92 FI Hybrid 'Ringo Deep Scarlet'.

## Miniature Varieties

**'Aerosol'** A single-flowered variety of the Bird's Egg type. Blooms are mauve with darker spots. There is also an 'Aerosol Improved'.

**'Barnham'** A bright orange-red double.

**'Cherry'** A scarlet and white double.

**'Cotton Tails'** It has lovely double white flowers. The foliage is light green with a zone.

**'Embassy'** It has very large flowers, single and scarlet-orange with a white eye. Tends to be almost of dwarf proportions and the blooms may be too large for its miniature size.

**'Frills'** An unusual flower formation with ragged, coral double blooms. The foliage is also unusual and appears to be near to the species type, *P.acetosum*.

**'Grey Sprite'**  A single with coral flowers. The small, stiff leaves have a narrow whitish to pink edging.

**'Gwen'**  Definitely not for the beginner. A tri-coloured Micro-miniature with single, bright scarlet flowers.

**'Red Black Vesuvius'**  It has nearly black foliage with a heavy zone. The blooms are single and scarlet. There is a 'Salmon Black Vesuvius'.

**'Red Spider'**  A Cactus type with dark red flowers.

**'Silver Kewense'**  A bi-colour with rather large leaves for a miniature and single, dark red flowers. It can be slow and difficult.

**'Tammy'**  Double scarlet flowers on a well-behaved plant. Easy for the beginner.

## Dwarf Varieties

**'Bird Dancer'**  This is a Stellar type with dark leaves and pretty, soft, single, spiky blooms.

**'Bridesmaid'**  Sometimes listed with Ornamental-leaved types. This has golden foliage and beautiful, soft, pale orange, double flowers.

**Dusky Rose'**  A rosebud with soft coral-pink flowers.

**'Fantasia'**  A double white.

**'Friesdorf'**  A primitive flower of currant red. It has dark well-zoned foliage and is a popular variety which may be found in garden centres.

**'Mr (Dr) Everaarts'**  A rose-pink double. It blooms well and is an easy one to try.

**'Sun Rocket'**  It has pea-green leaves and bright orange double flowers.

## Ivy-leaved Pelargoniums

**'Abel Carriere'**  This plant has semi-double blooms of Tyrian purple and is a stocky grower.

**'Balcon Royale'**  It has primitive-shaped flowers of blood-red and small foliage.

**'Barbe Bleue'**  A new double variety that is deepest purple to almost black.

**'Beauty of Eastbourne'**  A deep cerise-pink, semi-double.

**'Cornell'**  A compact plant with semi-double, dark lavender blooms.

**'Galilee'**  An old favourite with semi-double pink blooms.

**'Harlequin Mahogany'**  A double that is deepest red with stripes of white and shades.

**'La France'**  A popular semi-double lilac which is free-flowering.

**'Mexican Beauty'**  A semi-double with blooms of deep crimson.

**'Pink Rosebud'**  An 'Ivy-leaved' type with rosette-shaped flowers.

**'Red Cascade'**  The red variety of the 'Cascade' family. It has many primitive flowers. The small foliage makes it suitable for baskets and balconies in exposed places.

**'Rigi'**  A dark mauve, compact plant with semi-double flowers.

**'Rouletta' (synonym 'Mexicarin', 'Mexicano')**  An 'Ivy-leaved' with red and white striped flowers.

**'Snowdrift'**   A double with white flowers that are almost a rosette shape.

**'Snow Queen'**   This plant has floppy, double blooms of white with some markings in the top petals.

**'Sussex Lace'**   The leaves are netted with cream veins and it has semi-double pink blooms.

**'Tavira'**   A bright but soft red semi-double form.

**'Yale'**   A very dark, velvety red, semi-double.

## Miniature and Dwarf Ivy-leaved Varieties

**'Mini-Cascade'**   There are pink, red, rose and salmon blooms, all of small proportions and useful for hanging pot work. Single primitive flowers of repeat flowering habit.

**'Flakey'**   A cream, variegated Miniature. The flowers are small and whitish, with some mauve markings.

**'Gay Baby'**   Similar to the above but with shiny, green leaves.

**'Green Eyes'**   This plant just falls into this category. It is a mauve double with a greenish centre.

**'Lakeland'**   Another *Pelargonium* just in the Dwarf classification, but worth growing. It has golden-green foliage and double lavender blooms.

**'Sugar Baby' (synonym 'Pink Gay Baby')**   A Dwarf in habit. It has small, pretty, double flowers of pink. Flowers prolifically. Ideal for hanging pots.

*Fig 93 'Harlequin Pretty Girl' is a hybrid Ivy-leaved variety.*

## Hybrid Ivy-leaved Varieties

**'Blue Spring'**   As near to blue as soft lavender can be! A double, with quite large flowers and soft leaves.

**'Elsi'**   A variegated with creamy-gold leaves and double blooms that are orange.

**'Harlequin Pretty Girl'**   This plant has soft, large foliage and double flowers with orange and white stripes and shading.

**'Jack of Hearts'**   Soft pink with salmon tones.

**'Milfield Gem'**   A blush-pink double with upper petals that are marked with maroon.

**'Queen of Hearts'**   An off-white double with flowers that have streaks of deep pink and heart-shaped blotches on top petals. It can be tricky to grow, but worth a place in a collection.

**'Ten of Hearts'**   A semi-double with deep pink blooms.

# II GLOSSARY

**Annual**   Growing to maturity in one year or less.

**Anther**   The pollen-bearing part of the stamen.

**Awn**   Bristle-like growth.

**Calyx**   The outer flower part used to protect the single flower bud.

**Capsule**   Generally, the seed container.

**Carpel**   The part in which the seeds are formed.

**Chlorophyll**   The green pigment in plants which is essential for their survival. It is manufactured by the process of the plant absorbing light, then using the energy in the process of photosynthesis to build sugars from water and carbon dioxide.

**Cordate**   Heart-shaped.

**Cotyledon**   The first seedling leaves to appear.

**Crenate**   Used to describe a plant that has rounded teeth at leaf margin.

**Cultivar**   A cultivated variety.

**Entire**   Smooth, continuous edges to the leaf margin.

**Fertile**   Capable of producing seed.

**Fertilisation**   The fusing of male and female sex cells.

**Filament**   The anther's stalk.

**Genus (plural, genera)**   Botanical category of the classification of a group of plants with common characteristics evolved from, probably, a common ancestor and agreed by botanists.

**Geophyte**   A plant having an underground tuber for storing food.

**Glaucous**   Bluish tint caused by a bloom or waxy coating (patina), as on the skin of grapes.

**Habitat**   Home of plants in the wild.

**Hybrid**   A plant resulting from the crossing of two distinct types or species or sometimes genera.

**Inflorescence**   Arrangement of flowers, for example; spike, lavender; umbel, allium.

**Lanceolate**   Shaped like the head of a lance, in other words broad at the base, tapering to a point at the tip and at least three times as long as the width.

**Lobed**   A part of leaf or flower divided from the rest of the part, but not totally.

**Mericarp**   One of the five seeded portions.

**Node**   The place or joint where the leaf stalks meet the stem.

**Ovary**   The part of the lower end of the pistil containing the ovules or young seed.

**Palmate**   Hand-shaped, describing a leaf as an open hand.

**Pedicel**   Stalk of a single flower.

**Peduncle**   The stem supporting the flower arrangement.

**Peltate**   Joined to the middle.

**Perennial**   With a life-span of some years.

**Petiole**   Stalk of a leaf.

**Pip**   A single floret or flower.

**Pistil**   The female organ comprising an ovary, stigma and style (rostrum).

**Reniform**   Kidney-shaped.

**Rhizome**   Horizontal underground stem used for storage.

**Rib**   One of the main prominent leaf veins.

**Rostrum**   *see* **Style**.

**Serrated**   Saw-like teeth.

**Species**   A group of closely allied plants within a genus, having essential characteristics that are distinctive and consistently bred true to type from seed for generations.

**Sport**   This is a shoot differing from the host plant as a result of spontaneous change in its hereditary genes. In the wild, one cause could be the result of cosmic radiation. It can be simulated by man with the use of drugs and X-ray processes and in this way 'sporting' can be encouraged.

**Stamen**   The male element of a flower.

**Stigma**   The female element of a flower.

**Stipule**   Scales in pairs on the stem at the base of the petioles.

**Stolon**   This is the prostrate stem, rooting at the nodes.

**Style**   The stalk linking the ovary and the stigma.

*Fig 94* Pelargonium scandens. *An attractive species often growing to 4ft (120cm).*

**Sub-shrub**  Shrub-like plant where only the base is woody.
**Succulent**  Fleshy.
**Tomentose**  Covered with hairs.
**Tripartite**  Divided nearly to the base in three segments.

**Tuber**  Thickened fleshy root or underground stem for food storage.
**Umbel**  An inflorescence with all pedicels coming from the common centre, the top of the peduncle.

# Index

Note: Page numbers of illustrations are indicated in *italic* type.